SPIN GAME

EXPOSING POLITICAL LIES AND TACTICS

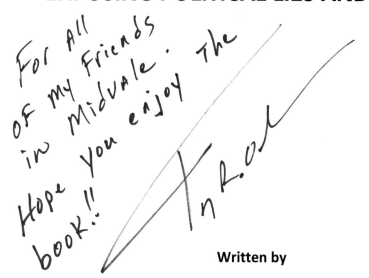

For All
of my Friends
in Midvale.
Hope You enjoy The
book!!

Written by

Tony Olson

FIRST EDITION

Red Stag Publishing
Regarding: Tony Olson
2001 NW Aloclek Drive
Suite #7
Hillsboro, OR 97124

First Printing: November 2014

Printed in the United States of America

ISBN: 978-0-9906030-0-9

Inquiries to: Redstagpublishing@outlook.com

Cover design by:
LG Grafix
Gilbert Loya
Lg_grafix@yahoo.com
Phone: 208-863-1073

" The hottest places in hell are reserved for those who, in the time of moral crisis, maintain their neutrality."

- Dante

Contents

ACKNOWLEDGEMENTS

First and foremost, I want to thank my wife, Justina, for convincing me that it was time to write a book. And, for putting up with all of the headaches, and the lost hours, that come along with it. Thank you for believing in me. You are my everything.

To Amanda and Payton, the best kids I could have ever dreamed of. You have both made me so proud. I wrote this book for you, hoping that someday you and your children can live in the America that I grew up in. The American dream is still out there. There is nothing you can't accomplish.

To my mother and father, who provided a wonderful life for me, and have continued to be an inspiration, even after death. You taught me nothing is impossible. Thank you for taking a chance and adopting me. I know I was a handful, but I think I turned out okay. I miss you.

To my biological mother, for doing the right thing. Thank you for not choosing the alternative. Take comfort in knowing I had an incredible life because of your selflessness. God bless you wherever you are.

To all of my relatives and friends. Your support has meant everything to me. I can safely say that I have the best group of friends in the world.

A very special thanks to Linda Stirling, for steering this ship in the right direction. You have been a mentor, a teacher, an inspiration, and a cheerleader. I could not have done this without your guidance. I'll turn your motto around a bit, as I say, "In all you do, *you* are the blessing."

To Gilbert Loya, the king of graphic design. You did a fantastic job of getting the vision onto the cover and website. Thank you for your talent and insight.

And to Tonja Cantrell, the fastest typist in the world. Thank you for getting all of my scribbling into a usable format. You saved me untold hours at the keyboard. You're the best.

And finally, I want to thank God for keeping me around a little longer. Apparently, he wants me here for a reason. Hopefully, this book is it. Otherwise, I'm all out of ideas.

Thank you for reading my book. God bless you all.

INTRODUCTION

I wrote this book hoping I could make a difference. Perhaps this is what I was meant to do. There have been a number of times I could have "met my maker", but didn't. I was adopted, not aborted. I've had brain surgery. And, I was only ten minutes removed from a shooting that killed three of my friends and wounded seven others (twenty-four total victims). I'm the lucky one. Every day is a blessing. Someone is looking out for me. Now, it is my turn to look out for others.

Over the course of the last six years, I have seen a cancer growing in this country. It's not the disease itself, but it affects just as many people, if not more. Like most cancers, it destroys its host from within. It attacks the brain, rendering it morally void. Symptoms include loss of common sense, difficulty understanding economics, and a desire to engage in class warfare. It often causes severe dependency, and feelings of acute entitlement. Long-term exposure can lead to paralysis . . . of the country. I, like many conservatives, am trying to find a cure.

Not that long ago, we admired hard work and individualism. We understood American exceptionalism. We celebrated those with vision and entrepreneurial spirit, and we celebrated their success. They built that success, and we knew it. We were never ashamed of our country, and we took a back seat to none. We took personal responsibility, and we faced each day with pride and dignity. As conservatives, we understood the value and the price of freedom. We were raised on qualities such as honesty, hard work, and respect. As children, we were taught to believe in ourselves and our capabilities. Racial tensions were dissolving and we knew there was more that bound us together than could ever separate us. If we had differences of opinion, we felt comfortable discussing them. We could laugh at our mistakes, but we also learned from them.

America was safe. We had the strongest military in the world. Terrorism was something that happened in other parts of the world, not here. We were living the American Dream, and we were never afraid to give credit to God. We understood America was founded according to Judeo-Christian principles, and those principles were never questioned.

After 238 years, America is still here. But sadly, things have changed, especially in the past few years. Many people today don't know the real America. The America they know is often based on information provided by the mainstream media, and Hollywood via social media. In either case, it's extremely biased. Liberal forums and social media are filled with anger, resentment, victimization, discrimination, and unfairness. The Left always has a problem, a victim, a crisis. The hate is constant. They have mastered the politics of envy and class warfare. They preach victimization and encourage an entitlement mentality. They engage in identity politics, pitting people against each other based on race, religion, gender, income, or sexual orientation. Now, everyone is a target: small businesses, corporations, banks, doctors, Tea Party members, insurance companies, oil companies, the coal industry, etc.

This systematic fragmentation is destroying the country. The Left has continued to turn Americans against each other for no other reason than to secure a voting base.

If people look closely, they can see the hypocrisy. The Left preaches open-mindedness but won't make the time, or effort, to research opposing views. They champion the poor publicly, while showing distain for them privately.

They claim Republicans are waging a "war on women," yet they fail to warn women about the dangers of abortion, and turn a blind eye to Sharia law, which allows beatings and honor killings of women and young girls, sexual mutilation, and child marriage.

They publically decry the condition of inner-city minorities, yet never seriously address the causes, because those people have become a reliable Democratic Party voting block, and their misfortune is viewed as acceptable collateral damage.

They talk about being responsible, but never take any responsibility. It's always someone or something else's fault, i.e. George Bush, Tea Party, weather, etc.

The Left expresses complete support for the Occupy Wall Street movements, whose only goal is to take from others. These are the same protestors responsible for numerous rapes and assaults, as well as defecating on cars and in common areas of public buildings.

That's where we are today. That's how our country is being run. Christianity and belief in the Constitution are considered "radical extremism." We are on a course toward financial, and moral, bankruptcy. We are the only ones who can change that. Dante once wrote, " The hottest places in hell are reserved for those who, in the time of moral crisis, maintain their neutrality."

The Media

A Gallup Poll, released in June 2014, showed that only eighteen percent of those polled had a great deal, or quite a lot, of confidence in TV news—an all-time low.

During that same period, Public Policy Polling conducted its annual poll, which asks TV viewers which news outlet they trust the most. *FOX News* has been the most trusted news source, by far, in all the polls to date. In the most recent poll, *FOX News* was trusted by thirty-five percent of viewers. The next most trusted news source was *PBS* at fourteen percent. *CNN* was third at ten percent, followed by *CBS* at nine percent. *MSNBC* and *Comedy Central* each had six percent, and *NBC* had three percent. Yes, as a trusted news source, *NBC* was beaten by *Comedy Central*.

Viewership for mainstream television news has been off by more than fifty percent at some networks. The blind allegiance to the current administration has forced many networks to report opinions, rather than facts. The facts that do get reported are often misrepresented or censored.

In the Press Freedom Index, the American media ranks forty-sixth world-wide, eight places below El Salvador.

The mainstream media has a history of bias. The Vietnam War, the DDT ban, Teddy Kennedy's Chappaquiddick incident, and the Monica Lewinski scandal, were all stories that magnified the bias. More recently, we have seen stories like Climategate, Fast and Furious, Occupy Wall Street, the IRS scandal, and the Benghazi attack, which have all been downplayed and under-reported by the mainstream media. It is no wonder their credibility continues to wane.

I also hold the Liberal media responsible for the deterioration of race relations in the United States. Creating hate crimes where there are none, and giving the current administration a pass with regard to racially divisive tactics (see: Trayvon Martin, Black Panther voter intimidation, etc., within these chapters), has resulted in a dramatic drop in the public's optimism of race relations.

Whether it's the economy, unemployment, foreign relations, climate change, crime, poverty, you name it, almost every story is spun in a more positive light for the Democrats, compared to the Republicans.

With the help of the media, the Left has been able to talk the talk without ever being accountable for not walking the walk.

The Sad State of the Union

In his campaign speeches, Barack Obama said that he would fundamentally transform the country. He certainly made good on that promise.

Gas, food, and utility costs are higher. Home ownership has declined. The number of people on food stamps has increased by forty-four percent. The labor-force participation rate is the lowest it's been in thirty-six years, and more than ninety-two million working-age Americans are unemployed, an increase of more than eleven million since Obama took office.

Of the jobs that have been "created" under Obama, most are part-time. The reported unemployment rate is just over six percent. However, the real unemployment rate, which counts people who have left the labor force because they can't find work, is almost double that number.

The poverty level, according to the Census Bureau, has remained above fifteen percent for three consecutive years—the first time since 1965. Social Security is cash-flow negative.

When Obama took office, America was coming out of a severe recession. Historically, the deeper the recession, the stronger the recovery. Obama should have enjoyed a robust recovery. Instead, this recovery has been anemic, at best. From 1982 to 2007, the economy sustained a rate of economic growth of 3.3 percent. Growth rates following a recession are generally much higher. Obama's best growth number was four percent in the second quarter of 2014, the first time it had broken three percent since he took office. Prior to that quarter, his high had been 2.8 percent. In contrast, Ronald Reagan had an average growth of 4.9 percent, with a high of seven percent.

Median household income has fallen by more than four percent. At the same time, the Consumer Price Index has increased by twelve percent. Discretionary income has taken a big hit.

The IRS, which was once just a necessary evil, has now become a political weapon. The NSA, who used to spy on other countries, now targets its own citizens.

Democrat leaders are divisive. They concentrate on differences and causes, rather than unity and solutions. They win elections through class warfare, aided by an incestuous relationship with the mainstream media. That relationship is powerful. How else would you get the black community to show ninety percent support, in 2012, to a president whose policies have decimated them, in particular, during his first term? How else would you convince seventy percent of the Jewish population in America to vote for a president who is hostile to Israel? You do it by misrepresenting, or completely avoiding, the facts.

The Democratic Party's Track Record

As the old saying goes "actions speak louder than words." Everybody talks a good game, but who really delivers?

President Obama and the Democrats have stated that income inequality is one of the most serious issues facing America today, that we need to put our trust in them to correct that injustice. So, how have the Democrats been doing on that issue?

Of the top fifty major cities with the worst income-inequality percentages, forty-seven are controlled by Democrats, including the top thirty-seven largest cities. The highest Republican-controlled city with income-inequality is Phoenix, at number thirty-eight.

Democrats also tell us their programs and leadership are far better at lifting people out of poverty. Well, the top ten major cities with the worst poverty percentages are all, once again, controlled by Democrats. They're led by Detroit, the poster child for the success of liberal policies.

What about gun control? Democrats are big on gun control and their cities have the strictest gun laws. So, it's the Republican controlled cities that have the most gun-related homicides, right? No. All of the top ten are Democrat-controlled cities (New Orleans, Detroit, Baltimore, Oakland, Newark, St. Louis, Miami, Richmond, Philadelphia, and Washington D.C.). If you count all gun-related deaths, including suicides and accidental shootings, the top ten are still one-hundred percent Democrat (except Oakland, Newark and Washington D.C. are out, and Las Vegas, Memphis and Cleveland are in).

Okay, let's look at overall crime. Surely, the tough crime stance taken by the Democrat leaders in the major cities has paid dividends. Of the top ten major cities with the highest overall crime rate, *nine* were controlled by Democrats. Oklahoma City (#9) prevented another clean sweep.

Finally, let's look at unemployment numbers. The top ten major metropolitan areas with the highest unemployment rates were also dominated by cities controlled by Democrats. The only top-ten city in this group, not controlled by Democrats, was Fresno.

By now, you should be starting to see a trend. Regardless of their intentions, the Democrats have done a poor job of keeping their own house in order.

The Wakeup Call

The last six years should have been a wakeup call for all Conservatives. When Obama won a second term in 2012, America was at a tipping point. Too many people were voting with their hearts, not with their heads, swayed by a media that perpetuated imaginary crises, and evoked public sympathy. That is not a game we need to play, nor do we need to compromise. We are the majority. Conservatives lose elections because we don't educate and we don't articulate. We will get more votes through unwavering principles and a well-articulated message than we ever will by compromising. If we follow some basic ground rules, we will increase our odds substantially.

First, all Republicans, moderate and conservative, need to be in this together. We all basically agree on the same set of principles. So there is no need to pander to the voting base subsets. It is time for all politicians to reacquaint themselves with the Constitution and the bible. A religiously-based conviction will not hurt you in the political arena. Stay true to your conservative principles.

Second, Republicans can't win a "he said, she said" argument with Democrats in the poll of public opinion. The Democrats will always have the mainstream media backing their narrative. If a Democrat says, "A minimum wage increase will help the poor", and all we say in rebuttal is "no, it will hurt the poor", then we will lose in the mind of the voter. However, if we provide facts showing how previous minimum-wage increases have caused massive job loss among the least-skilled, the disabled, minorities, etc., then we win that argument in the mind of the voter.

Everyone claims their platform is the one that will help the poor, the minorities, women, etc., but it is the conservative platform that actually can.

Many people's minds can be changed, but you need facts, and lots of them. Don't take a knife to a gunfight, when you have the option of taking a cannon. Help them understand the consequences and the benefits of both party's arguments. Give them enough facts to start a dialog. A hard-core Liberal will usually walk away. They have no tolerance for opposing viewpoints. An open-minded Independent will listen. Those are the people this book is written for, whether it comes directly from you, or from this book.

Finally, we all need to be on the same page. Republicans are notorious for being "all over the place" on the same issues. This is one area where the Democrats are masters. Regardless of how ridiculous the narrative, the Democrats always stick to the same talking points. It projects unity, and if everyone is saying the same thing, it is more likely to be believed and retained. Imagine what we can do with actual facts.

Get a set of talking points on each subject. Everyone, politicians or not, needs to be consistent with their facts. Talking points are now the weapon of choice in today's political environment. There are many in this book. Keep it handy. Democrats don't empower their followers. We can.

America needs an opposition party that is prepared and willing to fight for its heart and soul. Stick to the Conservative platform. Don't worry about trying to sway minority voters. There are more conservative minority voters than you think. The others will always vote Democrat . . . until they learn the facts. Our job is to put the facts in their hands.

CHAPTER ONE

Political Identity

Republicans and Democrats offer two distinct visions of what's right for America. The Democratic platform is generally liberal, and the Republican platform is generally conservative. However, not everyone fits neatly into the category of Republican or Democrat, and many people are confused with regard to party platforms when it comes time to vote. Therefore, it is particularly important that each person does his or her own independent research to determine what political choices will best meet their vision for the future of the country.

Throughout our lives, our political opinions are shaped in a variety of ways. Our first exposure to politics was usually through the opinions of our parents or other family members, when we were children. Once we got older, we often rejected our parent's political views, out of rebellion, only to return years later, once we realized our parents were smarter than we thought.

Geography also plays a role in our political indoctrination. Different parts of the country have different political leanings. Rural areas are generally very conservative, while large metropolitan areas are usually more liberal. The attitudes of those around us play a big role in how our political outlook is shaped.

Schools, especially today, have become more of a political incubator. Unfortunately, the majority of academia espouses a liberal mindset and political correctness, rather than teaching students to be open-minded, independent, critical thinkers.

Often, political affiliation is the result of greed or self-interest. Those on government assistance will usually vote for the party that wants to expand social programs.

Many political attitudes are based on race, religion, or sexual orientation. People often vote based on the voting preferences of their respective sub-groups, without regard to the party's historical effect on that sub-group. African-Americans overwhelmingly vote the Democratic Party ticket, despite the negative economic impact Democrat policies have had on their community. Many Catholics vote Democrat, despite the fact that many parts of the Democrat platform run contrary to basic Catholic beliefs.

The final source of political influence is the media. This is probably the most common source, as well as the most unreliable. Let me be very clear on this—most of the news reported in the media is biased and incomplete. You are being given bits and pieces of news based on the political agendas of those respective news outlets. On a world-wide basis, the freedoms and trust-worthiness of our news agencies rank incredibly low. Between the media spin and political misrepresentations, it is hard for many to identify with a party. As a result, you'll find a significant number of uninformed voters who vote based on single issues, rather than the overall value of a respective party's platform. Historically, the Left has relied on single-issue voters, because single-issue voters are easier to manipulate.

Overall, we have many influences that shape our political mindset. More often than not, the pieces of this puzzle are based on opinions or political agendas, rather than facts. The purpose of this book is to bypass the other sources of political influence, and provide the facts on a number of political issues, enabling you to make informed political decisions.

I am writing this book as a Conservative. As a former Democrat, I have seen the issues from both perspectives. The parties used to bear some similarities, but things have changed over time. The old "blue dog" Democrats of the past made decisions that go against today's liberal ideology. For example, John F. Kennedy, a Democrat, is one of the most well-liked presidents of all time. Based on many of his policies and decisions, Kennedy would have been considered a Republican today. He believed in peace through strength. And, unlike the current president, he took full responsibility for everything done under his watch. He argued for reduced taxes and a balanced budget. Kennedy once stated. "I am in favor of a tax cut because I'm concerned we are going to have an increase in unemployment, and we may move into a period of economic downturn. I think this tax cut can give the stimulus to our economy over the next two or three years." That rationale is absolutely correct. But, it is the polar opposite of today's Democratic stance. Someone in the Kennedy administration understood economics. Kennedy also showed strength in dealing with foreign policy, and never apologized to other countries for American exceptionalism.

I can tell you, without hesitation, the only way we are going to get this country back on track is through conservative principles. This country was built on conservative principles, and that's how it will be saved. The majority of Americans identify themselves as Conservatives, contrary to what the media wants you to believe. Collectively, we have the power to keep America moving in the right direction.

Conservative Majority

There are a number of reasons why Republicans lose elections, and being a minority party is not one of them. In November 2013, A George Washington University Battleground Poll showed that fifty-six percent of Americans identify themselves as "very conservative" or "somewhat conservative", while only thirty-eight percent identified themselves as "very liberal" or "somewhat liberal." In fact, every Battleground Poll taken in the last fourteen years, for a total of twenty-two polls, has shown Conservatives are the overwhelming majority in America.

Every Gallup Poll taken since 2000 shows Conservatives outnumber Liberals in almost every state. And, Survey USA, which compiles polling data throughout the United States, shows Conservatives easily outnumber Liberals, even in many traditionally Liberal cities and states. There are many "closet Conservatives" in academia and the media who are afraid to self-identify as Conservatives out of fear that doing so may jeopardize their careers.

This is nothing new. We have always been predominantly conservative as a country. This becomes more evident when we have a solid conservative candidate. In 1984, Ronald Reagan was re-elected by a landslide, taking forty-nine states and ninety-eight percent of the electoral votes.

In contrast, in 2012, Barack Obama won his re-election by a margin of less than four percent of the popular vote, carried only twenty-six states, and garnered only sixty-two percent of the Electoral College. Mitt Romney lost because he came across as being somewhat moderate, and did not fire up the Conservative base. He obviously got the Mormon vote, but several million evangelicals chose not to vote. A candidate like Reagan would have won that election.

Most Conservatives consider themselves "Fiscal Conservatives" rather than "Social Conservatives." Those identifying as "Social Conservatives" list abortion as their primary social concern. It is usually social issues that the media and pollsters use to mislead the public. For example, a Gallup Poll, released in May 2014, showed that forty-seven percent of Americans consider themselves to be "pro-choice", and forty-six percent considered themselves "pro-life." However, the same poll showed that fifty-nine percent thought abortion should be either illegal, or legal only in the case of rape, incest, or when the life of the mother is in danger, which is basically a "pro-life" stance. A *CNN* poll taken two months prior, showed identical results.

A *CBS* Poll, released in July 2013, showed that sixty-one percent of those polled wanted more limits on abortion.

In June 2014, a Gallup Poll was released which asked respondents to rate their confidence in American institutions. Those having the highest degree of confidence were the military, small business, the police, churches, and medical institutions. Those who were given the least amount of confidence were Congress, TV news, internet news, big business, unions, and newspapers. Obviously, the bulk of the institutions receiving the worst ratings are controlled by the Left, a fact which Gallup forgot to mention.

As public schools have continued their slide to the Left over the years, the confidence level in them has faded dramatically. A Gallup Poll taken in 1975 showed that sixty-two percent of respondents had a "great deal" or "quite a lot" of confidence in public schools. The latest Gallup Poll shows that level of confidence has dropped to twenty-six percent.

Confidence in television news, which is predominantly liberal-biased, has dropped from forty-seven percent in 1973 to only eighteen percent in the latest Gallup Poll.

In a recent Lifeway Research poll, eighty-five percent of Americans voted to keep the words "under God" in the Pledge of Allegiance. Only eight percent wanted the words removed. An earlier *NBC* poll found that eighty-six percent of Americans were in favor keeping "under God" in the Pledge of Allegiance.

What these polls show is that, as these institutions have become more Liberal, Americans have become less trusting and less confident in them. This is another clear indication that the majority of Americans are Conservative.

Republicans

Republicans are the party of the middle class and working class. Most Republicans have a high-school diploma and some college education. Seventeen percent more members of middle-class families ($30,000 - $75,000) vote Republican. Twenty-two percent more of the white working-class votes Republican. The working poor also tend to vote Republican. Farmers and small business owners vote Republican, as do manufacturing and construction workers. Those who understand foreign policy and national defense vote Republican, such as most military personnel, engineers, and national security experts. Doctors voted for Republicans in 2012 by a nineteen-point margin. Nurses and married women also vote Republican.

Those who started with nothing and worked their way up the ladder to become rich, usually vote Republican. Trust-fund babies, who did not earn their fortunes, do not. People who had to work hard for their money, and those who are thrifty with their money, vote Republican.

Republicans believe in God, and God is mentioned numerous times in their platform. Democrats removed God from their platform during the 2012 Democrat National Committee meeting. It was added back to the platform, only after public outcry, but is only mentioned once. Most of the Democrats in attendance booed when the word "God" was added back in.

Conservatives are generally of the opinion that charity should be a personal decision, not a government mandate, and each of us are personally responsible for helping those in need. Charity is a genuinely benevolent act. When you give that responsibility to the government, you lose the ability to determine who is truly in need and who is simply looking for a handout and taking advantage of the situation. Those who are truly in need should get more help. Those looking for a handout should get nothing. And it is the responsibility of each individual who is successful to do their part to help provide for those less fortunate. As such, charity is a creature of the Right. Republicans give more to charity than Democrats by a two-to-one margin.

Republicans value self-reliance and individualism. Welfare should be given to people to help them gain independence, and only given to those who are not capable of supporting themselves. Long-term welfare should only be provided to those who are physically unable to become self-reliant.

Republicans believe government should not control healthcare. Uninsured individuals should be addressed within a privatized healthcare system. A competitive, free-market system would give consumers more choices and encourage competitive pricing.

Republicans believe in school choice. Voucher programs create competition and give many underprivileged children an opportunity to attend better schools.

Republicans value personal and property rights over environmental regulation. Natural resources should be used, if managed properly. Green energy should be left to private businesses to develop, and only used by the consumer when those resources become economically feasible.

Conservatives respect the Constitution and the law of the land as it was written, and believe state and local governments are able to make better decisions than the Federal Government. Our rights and freedoms are second to none. Republicans believe in free speech, even if it offends. They see political correctness as a handicap. They embrace American exceptionalism, and honor traditional family values. Republicans see the United States as the greatest nation on earth.

Democrats

Democrats are the party of the rich. They are also the party of the non-working poor, who have become dependent on government assistance. Seventy-five percent of the richest families, and sixty percent of the twenty richest Americans, are Democrats. The super-rich are generally Democrat by almost a 2-1 margin. In blue states (Democrat), the average income is about $100,000. In red states (Republican), the average income is only about $30,000. People with advanced degrees and those without a high-school diploma are generally Democrat.

Those who inherited their wealth are generally Democrat. Trust-fund babies are Democrat. Democrats represent the wealthiest congressional districts, and the biggest political campaign contributors. The biggest donors to the Democratic Party are lawyers, followed by government unions, government bureaucrats, teachers, and union members.

Eighty percent of the lawyers in congress are Democrat, but only one-in-six doctors in congress are Democrat.

Democrats want a large federal government, with only limited state and local control—a government-regulated economy.

Democrats claim to be the protectors of the poor, and think government needs to play a larger role in helping the less fortunate, because there is not enough charity to go around. Democrats support a welfare state, even for those who are able to work. They believe welfare protects the poor and brings fairness, and as such, the rich need to be taxed more to support the poor.

Liberals don't see America as the greatest nation on earth. They believe the most successful, prosperous nations in the world are liberal democracies. They think world peace can be obtained through appeasement and apology, with no show of strength. Liberals believe terrorism is the result of arrogant U.S. foreign policy, and the best way to deal with terrorism is through diplomacy.

Democrats see man as inherently good, and any wrong-doing must be society's fault. They espouse tolerance of all lifestyles and beliefs, including Islamic Sharia Law. Democrats view all cultures as equal, even those with religious intolerance and gender inequality.

Democrats think government should allocate more money toward public schools, while reducing class size and increasing teacher salaries. They are against school choice at the behest of the teachers' unions, apparently willing to sacrifice a quality education for job security for many marginal teachers.

Democrats view the Constitution as outdated, and think they can make better decisions for others, than others can make for themselves. They only believe in free speech that does not offend, i.e. political correctness. Democrats see society as distinct groups, i.e. white versus black, rich versus poor, male versus female, etc. As such, the Left promotes envy and victimization, eventually demanding additional rights or compensation. The Left sees the world as being perpetually broken, always having something that needs to be repaired or changed.

Democrats generally see religion as being of little importance. To them, religion is a private matter, separate from government. They think all references to God should be removed from public and government property.

The Issues

The following issues are considered "hot button" issues between the Republicans and the Democrats. I have provided some of each party's respective stances on these issues. Read these carefully, then, read them again after you have finished the book. I believe you will have a much different outlook the second time.

Climate Change

Republican View - Republicans will approve of green energy when it becomes affordable. Forcing people to abandon fossil fuels, and reduce carbon emissions will increase their cost of living substantially, but does nothing to impact the climate. Republicans believe climate change is a natural cycle, and human activity has no significant effect on the climate. The proof is overwhelming.

Democrat View - Global warming is real and is caused by increased carbon dioxide due to the burning of fossil fuels (coal, oil, and natural gas). There is a consensus among scientists, based on hundreds of computer models. Arctic and Antarctic ice is melting rapidly and sea levels are rising. Democrats want excessive regulations on businesses in order to "protect" our people and the environment.

Racism

Republican View - Republicans believe in equal rights for all citizens, regardless of race or gender. Everyone should be given equal opportunities. No one should be given special opportunities. Affirmative action is a form of reverse racism. People should be admitted to schools, and employed, based on qualifications and ability, not the color of their skin.

Democrat View – Republicans are racist. Racism is responsible for inequality and lack of opportunities within the African-American community. Affirmative action regulations are necessary to provide those opportunities. Blacks have prospered, and race relations have improved, under Democrat leadership.

Gun Control

Republican View - Republicans believe in the right to defend themselves, both as a country and as an individual, and we believe in the right to arm ourselves accordingly. Gun control only increases gun violence and overall violent crime. Gun control laws will only keep guns out of the hands of law-abiding citizens. Criminals will always have access to guns. Guns don't kill people, people kill people.

Democrat View - More guns mean more violence. People should be protected by law enforcement agencies and the military. Stricter gun laws are needed to eliminate gun violence, stop accidental shootings, and keep criminals from having access to guns. Guns kill people, period.

Immigration

Republican View - Republicans want a secure border. Illegal immigration has led to increased crime, and the introduction and spread of third-world diseases. It has increased the burden on U.S. taxpayers and reduced employment opportunities for native workers. Republicans oppose amnesty for those who are here illegally. We believe existing immigration laws should be enforced and would like to enhance the guest-worker program.

Democrat View - Illegal immigrants should receive amnesty, as well as all educational and health benefits that U.S. citizens are allowed to have, regardless of legal status or ability to pay. American is a nation of immigrants. Immigrants accept jobs that American workers won't do. There is no reason that immigrants, legal or illegal, should not be accepted.

Minimum Wage

Republican View – Minimum wage regulations reduce job opportunities for those who need them the most. Prior minimum wage increases have cost millions of jobs. Minimum wage is a "learning wage", not a "living wage." Job creation and a solid economy in a free-market environment will increase wages for everyone. North Dakota is a prime example of this.

Democrat View – Minimum wage is a "living wage." Millions of people need a minimum wage increase to lift them out of poverty. Employers should be willing to increase their cost of doing business, or raise prices, to allow for higher wages. Employees should be paid a minimum wage, even if they are unable to provide that level of production to the employer.

Jobs/Unemployment

Republican View - Republicans believe the best way to create jobs and improve the economy is to let successful people continue to be successful and grow businesses. We believe in reducing government regulations and lowering taxes. It's our mandate to create a "business friendly" environment. We believe the highest standard of living and the most opportunities are created in a free-market society. Job creation and unemployment numbers under the current administration are bad. The public is being misled.

Democrat View – The current administration has turned the economy and unemployment around. President Obama has created millions of jobs and the economy is solid. Increases in regulations, higher business tax rates, health care mandates, and an increased minimum wage, will have little effect on business success and unemployment.

Income Inequality

Republican View- Republicans seek equal opportunities rather than equal outcomes. People make different choices with regard to education, employment, family structure, work hours, and geography, all of which determine their respective income. If all variables are taken into account, the actual degree of income inequality is minimal.

Democrat View - There is a large degree of income inequality between the poor and the rich, whites and blacks, women and men. The rich need to pay more to provide for those with low income. Personal choices of low-income individuals should not be a factor. Regulations need to be enacted to ensure that all Americans are more equal financially.

Abortion

Republican View – Republicans are against abortion, either entirely, or only in the cases of rape, incest, or danger to the life of the mother. Scientists agree life begins at conception. If a mother does not want the child, adoption is the ethical alternative. Contraception is an acceptable choice to prevent unwanted pregnancy. Republicans oppose tax-payer funded abortion.

Democrat View – Democrats are in favor of abortion under virtually all circumstances. A fetus is not a human, and does not have rights. Termination of an unborn child is morally acceptable. Abortion is a safe procedure, with no proven physical or psychological health risks. Government should provide taxpayer-funded abortions for women who cannot afford them.

War on Women

Republican View - Republicans believe women are biologically different than men. Women should be respected for the career decisions they make based on those biological differences. There is a small income gap between men and women, but it's based on career choices, risk levels, and amount of hours worked. Democrat policies are far more detrimental to women than those of Republicans.

Democrat View – The Republicans are waging a "war on women." There is a big income gap between women and men, for which the Republicans are responsible. Women only make seventy-seven cents for every dollar a man makes. Republicans are against equal rights for women. The Republican stance on reproductive rights also shows they are against women.

Conclusion

Each of the issues mentioned above has a dedicated chapter in this book. I have done extensive research to give you the facts on each subject. These facts will give you all the information you need to make an informed decision when it comes time to vote.

You are likely to be upset when you discover what's happening in America. I'm just the messenger.

First and foremost, Republicans should not try to emulate the Democrats. It's obvious that a majority of Americans are Conservative. Why are so many Republican politicians reluctant to stand on a conservative platform? Voters who want Democrat policies will vote for Democrats. America now, more than ever, needs an opposition party. It's quite simple . . . conservative policies have worked, liberal policies have not. Liberalism and socialism have never been successful, anywhere.

Good ideas have come from all political parties, and we need a multi-party system for the purpose for which it was intended, to act as a checks-and-balance mechanism, and to provide a variety of ideas and options. That being said, the conservative platform is still the best for the majority of Americans.

Republicans are letting the media define them, without any pushback. Conservatives must do a better job of getting their message to the masses. We need a concise, articulated message, with no apologies for our beliefs. Republicans have got to learn the facts and be able to articulate them to the uninformed voters. This includes using consistent talking points.

The following chapters will give you a wealth of information on nine crucial issues. These facts will provide direction and give you the ammunition needed to easily debunk the media spin. Whether you are a politician, political activist, ordinary citizen, or patriot, you need to learn this information. It will make a difference. God bless you all. Enjoy the rest of the book.

CHAPTER TWO

Climate Change

For years there have been alternating predictions of catastrophic global warming and cooling, rising sea levels, and various impending weather disasters, all of which have failed to materialize. As more data has become available, it has become increasingly clear the temperatures and weather patterns that we are currently experiencing globally are well within the historic natural variation of the earth's climate system. Despite the media hysteria, we are in a period of relatively moderate climate.

Unfortunately, the integrity of climate research has been compromised by ideological, financial, and political interests. The supposed "evidence" of man-made climate impact continues to change as it is proven false, yet the climate alarmists continue to invoke visions of impending environmental catastrophe.

This chapter presents an overwhelming amount of evidence that easily debunks the myth of anthropogenic (man-made) climate change, and cannot be successfully challenged.

Yes, there have been periods of global warming and global cooling throughout history . . . and there will continue to be. But, there is no evidence whatsoever that man has caused any of it. No man-made warming has yet been detected that is distinct from naturally-occurring warming patterns.

The earth's temperature has fluctuated for thousands of years. Our current temperature is below the average temperature in the past 3000 years. The warmest period in recent recorded history was the Medieval Warm Period (800-1200 A.D), when temperatures were seven to nine degrees warmer than today. At one point in our history, the earth was tropical from pole to pole. Tropical plant and animal fossils have been found both in Antarctica and on the Island of Spitsbergen in the Arctic Ocean.

This chapter was originally titled "Global Warming", but before I could get it completed, the climate alarmists had changed their rally cry, due to a lack of evidence supporting any real warming. The fact that this chapter even needs to be written is a testament to the power of media spin and the lack of critical thinking among the masses on this issue.

Those of us who have been around for fifty or so years remember another such apocalyptic prophecy . . . Global Cooling.

In the 1970s the media and politicians were all on the bandwagon with the "science experts" who claimed we were well on our way to the next Ice Age. *Newsweek* and *Time* magazines both published articles warning of impending doom, and urged readers to stockpile food and eliminate the use of aerosols. When the cooling failed to materialize, *Newsweek* found it necessary to print a correction, albeit thirty-one years later, stating that they were "so spectacularly wrong about the near-term future." They weren't the only ones who were wrong. Numerous books, newspaper articles, speeches, magazine articles, scientific papers, and television reports were all relegated to the fiction section.

At that point, most journalists would have tucked their tails (or tales) between their legs and went home, forever scarred by the embarrassment that comes with epic failure. Instead, they simply manufactured a new crisis . . . man-made Global Warming. This may be the single biggest hoax in history. While I agree there have been, and always will be, periods of warming and cooling, evidence shows unequivocally that man's ability to cause or prevent climate change is insignificant.

The claim of a human-caused climate crisis is based upon speculative theories, contrived data, and unproven modeling predictions. All empirical evidence suggests nature controls the climate, not man.

Once you understand the science and empirical data, it becomes clear man's impact on climate is almost non-existent.

The primary focus in the scientific debate on man-made climate change is the sensitivity of our climate to increasing levels of carbon dioxide in the atmosphere, known as climate sensitivity. Climate sensitivity relates changes in surface temperatures to changes in the warming influence of greenhouse gases and other factors that affect the earth's radiation balance. The belief is this: if climate sensitivity is high, then significant warming could be expected in the future. If climate sensitivity is low, the future warming will be lower.

There are three primary methods for estimating climate sensitivity: 1) instrumental observations, 2) Paleoclimate data, and 3) General Circulation Models (GSM) simulations. Estimates based on instrumental observations, especially those based on warming data over an extended time frame, are superior by far.

The "evidence" for human-caused climate change cited by the alarmists is based on General Circulation Models, i.e. climate models, which have yet to be proven accurate. Not one of the thousands of climate models created accurately predicted our current seventeen-year span of zero temperature increase. Man may be predictable, but Mother Nature is not.

Of the warming that has occurred since 1850, approximately seventy percent occurred prior to 1940. As such, the claim that a post-World War II industrial build-up is responsible for carbon emissions that lead to global warming, is baseless.

Still, every alarmist, including media outlets, politicians, environmentalists, and even Al Gore, use the climate assessment reports of the Intergovernmental Panel on Climate Change (IPCC), which are based almost solely on climate models, to present their case. Thousands of scientists disagree with the findings of the IPCC, and every IPCC report to date has been debunked. Keep in mind, the IPCC is a political body, not a scientific body. The scientists who contribute to the reports are likely to have a vested interest, either ideologically or financially, in the conclusions reached by the reports. I will discuss the IPCC in more detail a bit later in this chapter.

The Media

If factual scientific data had been reported by the media two decades ago, the subject of man-made global warming would not even be an issue today. Unfortunately, the bulk of the mainstream media has been conditioned to accept the deceptive reporting of human-caused climate change without question. The days of unbiased news are becoming a distant memory, as are the days of the critical thinking, investigative journalist. A recent survey found that eighty-nine percent of the journalists surveyed used internet blogs and social media sites for their resources, due to time constraints. This may offer a partial explanation of why the media has been so incredibly wrong on all things environmental. However, the larger problem lies in the media's tendency to follow a strict ideology. Following that ideology leads to overwhelming bias. For example, climate writer Russell Cook recently reported he had chronicled the broadcast transcripts for the *PBS News Hour*, with regard to global warming, over an eighteen-year period. During that period, there were approximately 400 instances where global warming was discussed. The program only mentioned evidence critical of global warming five times, four of which were very brief. One percent!! That is what they describe as "fair and balanced." I would like to think that is the exception, not the norm. Unfortunately, it is not.

Over the years, the media has bombarded us with dire predictions of environmental catastrophes in the making. It was predicted that the ice caps would be completely gone by 2012, and eventually polar bears would become extinct. We now have record ice packs and the polar bear population has increased over 500 percent since the mid-60s. In his 1968 best-selling book, *The Population Bomb*, Dr. Paul Ehrlich predicted major food shortages and hundreds of millions of deaths by starvation in the 1970s. He also predicted that by 1980 "All important animal life in the sea will be extinct." Despite this obvious failure to predict properly, Ehrlich and those like him are the kinds of people the media still calls upon as their "experts" when doing a news story on climate change. The public, however, is catching on. More and more people are opting to do their own research, while opinion-based sources like *CNN* and *MSNBC* are losing a huge percentage of viewers, as well as a great deal of credibility. News outlets will soon find it necessary to abandon opinion and concentrate on obtaining and printing factual information, if they wish to remain a viable entity. History has a way of coming back to bite those who cry wolf. Here are a few examples of headlines over the past few decades. It's disturbing to see how easily one crisis is replaced by another, once it is debunked.

Science: Another Ice Age? (*Time Magazine,* November 13, 1972)

Another Ice Age? (*Time Magazine,* June 24, 1974)

The Big Freeze (*Time Magazine,* January 31, 1977)

Earth at the Tipping Point: Global Warming Heats Up (*Time Magazine,* March 26, 2006)

The Global Warming Survival Guide (*Time Magazine,* April 9, 2007)

Climate Change Could Sink Statue of Liberty, Report Warns (*Time Magazine,* May 20, 2014)

SPIN GAME

Is Mankind Manufacturing a New Ice Age for Itself? (*L.A. Times,* January 13, 1970)

Scientist Sees Chilling Signs of New Ice Age (*L.A. Times,* September 24, 1972)

Scientists warn of Global Warming's Abrupt Changes (*L.A. Times,* March 18, 2014)

Climate Change: While We Fiddle, the World Burns...and floods and parches (*L.A. Times,* March 26, 2014)

Ice Age Around the Corner (*The Chicago Tribune,* July 10, 1971)

Ice Age, Worse Food Crises' Seen (*The Chicago Tribune,* October 30, 1974)

B-r-r-r: New Ice Age On Way Soon? (*The Chicago Tribune,* March 2, 1975)

The Ice Age Cometh: The System That Controls Our Climate (*The Chicago Tribune,* April 13, 1975)

A Solution for Global Warming (*The Chicago Tribune,* August 8, 2013)

Global Warming Threatens More Deadly Everest-like Avalanches: Report (*The Chicago Tribune,* May 20, 2014)

Threat From Global Warming Heightened: U.N. Report (*The Chicago Tribune,* March 31, 2014)

How far will the media go to fuel the hysteria? A recent article in *Mother Jones* claims global warming will lead to 180,000 more rapes, 22,000 additional murders, and 3.5 million assaults, over the next ninety years. *NBC's* Ann Curry claims global warming leads to increased stress levels in pre-teen children. Another report states global warming increases infidelity. The list goes on and on. Ask yourself this: when was the last time these news outlets were right?

Weather Extremes—A Media Fantasy

NBC News recently aired a prime time documentary that could only be described as a climate alarmism extravaganza. The documentary *Ann Curry Reports: Our Year of Extremes—Did Climate Change Just Hit Home?* doubles down on alarmist claims that have already proven to be false. Curry states that there is virtually no debate among climate scientists that climate change is real and "largely caused by human activity." Curry went on to say that climate change is "A humanitarian crisis of epic proportions" and "we owe it to our children to put policies aside and weigh the latest scientific evidence for ourselves."

Apparently, weighing scientific evidence is not one of Ann's stronger attributes. Nor is it for the *Huffington Post*, who published an article praising the documentary, and chastising some of the other networks (like *CNN* and *MSNBC*) for not doing similar reports.

Perhaps the other networks did weigh the scientific evidence, or maybe they are realizing what happens when you push the spin button too many times (*CNN* and *MSNBC* have both lost almost fifty percent of their viewership).

Had Ms. Curry done her homework, she would have found that most real climate scientists feel man has little, if any, impact on climate change. And, that the so-called evidence cited in the IPCC reports, that journalists so often reference, is based solely on climate models which have proven to be inaccurate. She would have also discovered there has been no warming in the last seventeen years, and that the first five IPCC reports have already been debunked. As for the claim that 2013 was a "year of extreme weather", it was actually an extremely calm weather year. There were only 771 tornadoes in 2013, the lowest number since 2000, and well below average (2011 had 1894 tornadoes and 2004 had 1820 tornadoes). The number of wild fires (40,306) were down from 2102 (67,774) and 2011 (74,126), and were the lowest in over a decade. The number of 100-degree days in the U.S. was the lowest on record. And hurricanes saw one of the weakest years in recent history. The U.S. has not seen a category three, four, or five hurricane since 2005—the longest period since the civil war.

There were only seven weather and climate disasters in the U.S. in 2013, and all of them were in the central part of the country. Both the east and west coasts had none. This number was down from eleven in 2012 and fourteen in 2011. The Climate Extremes Index from NOAA shows weather extremes were below average in 2013.

All of these facts are readily available to any investigative journalist. Unfortunately, the U.S. is experiencing a shortage of investigative journalists.

The mainstream media continues to claim increasing violent storm activity resulting from man-made climate change, and demands immediate action, despite the fact that global storm activity is at historic lows. The U.S. is also experiencing relatively mild weather, regardless of what the media tries to tell you.

The media is quick to point out record drought conditions in California, but fails to mention that Michigan and North Dakota each had the wettest year on record in 2013. Alaska had its third wettest year in 2013, and the lower 48 had the 21st wettest year on record.

The media immediately reports unusually high temperatures, complete with forecasts of "continued global warming" and impending doom, but somehow fails to mention that 2013 had the fewest number of 100-degree days on record in the U.S., and that the number of high temperature records in the U.S. dropped by approximately sixty percent from 2012 to 2013. For the first time in over a decade, the number of record low temperatures exceeded the number of record high temperatures, and 2013 was only the 37th warmest year in the 119-year period of record. And, in case you were wondering, the five years with the most 100-degree days in the U.S. were 1930, 1934, 1936, 1954, and 1980. None were even in the last thirty years.

There has been little, if any, global warming since 1979 if non-greenhouse influences like *El Nino* events are excluded.

Global drought conditions have not heightened. A paper published by the journal *Nature* in 2012 found "little change in global drought over the past sixty years." Even the IPCC determined there is "not enough evidence at present to suggest more than a low confidence in a global-scale observed trend in drought."

Wild weather was actually more common during colder periods in the earth's history. A paper published January 21, 2014 in Quaternary Science Reviews reconstructs storm activity in Iceland over the past 1,200 years and finds storm activity and extreme weather variability was far more common during the Little Ice Age as compared to the Medieval Warm Period and the 20th Century.

Weather is ruled by various solar activity, topography, and oceanic influences. Wild weather is usually caused by extreme differences in air pressure and temperature, which produce strong winds as the atmosphere equalizes.

Despite the media's best attempt to instill fear in our minds with regard to extreme weather conditions, the evidence proves them wrong. Hurricanes and tornadoes have become less frequent and severe (although they get more media coverage), and meteorological experts agree that no increase in storms has occurred outside of a natural variation of the climate system.

Sorry, Ann. Your story made for good fiction, but little else. By the way, aren't you the same Ann Curry who tried to link pre-teen children's stress levels to the effects of climate change in 2007? The same Ann Curry who cited Mt. Kilimanjaro as an example of global warming-related ice melt in 2008? I thought so.

That Pesky Antarctic Ice

On Tuesday, May 13, 2014 the main-stream media came alive with front-page stories of irreversible, catastrophic Antarctic Ice melt. "A rise of ten feet or more", claimed the *New York Times*, "four feet or more", stated *USA Today*. Not to be outdone, Brian Williams, on *NBC Nightly News*, raised the projection to thirteen feet. The hysteria centered around reports done by two groups of "scientists" who analyzed data on the West Antarctic Ice shelf. One group, from the University of California, stated that the West Antarctic ice shelf had "gone into irreversible retreat." The other group, from the University of Washington, determined it was "too late to stabilize the ice sheet." They used "sophisticated computer modeling," to come to their conclusions.

Before you start building that ark, let's take a look at some very cold, hard facts. The West Antarctic ice shelf is a region comprising only about eight percent of the ice covering Antarctica. Within that region, there are two glaciers that are sliding down into the sea, which has been happening steadily with most glaciers since the end of the Ice Age, some 18,000 years ago, without any help from mankind. These two glaciers account for about ten percent of the West Antarctic Ice Shelf, but less than one percent of the total Antarctic ice. Just two weeks prior to the release of these reports, Antarctic sea ice reached record levels, covering 3.5 million square miles. That beat the old record in April, 2008 by 124,000 square miles, and the ice coverage was continuing to increase. In June,2014 Southern hemisphere sea ice reached record coverage, and sea ice globally stood at 1.005 million square kilometers above average.

Just five months prior to the reports, Antarctica had the lowest temperature ever recorded on earth at -135.8°F. Within days of that record low temperature, a team of climate scientists, on an expedition to document the effects of global warming in the region, got stuck in the Antarctic ice pack and had to be rescued by an ice breaker and a helicopter. Subsequently, the ice breaker also got stuck. The Antarctic ice at that time was covering more than 300,000 square miles more than the prior thirty-year average. If parts of West Antarctica are indeed melting, East Antarctica is more than making up for it.

Glaciers have been growing and receding for thousands of years. Scientists know of at least thirty-three separate periods when glaciers grew and receded. In many cases, reduction in ice and snow mass was actually due to lower precipitation levels, not global warming.

But what if the alarmists are right, and temperatures increase globally by as much as five degrees over the next hundred years? That would raise the average annual temperature in Antarctica to a balmy minus fifty-one degrees.

I am having trouble rationalizing how vast quantities of ice can melt on a continent that has an average annual temperature of -56°F, when sea water freezes at +28°F. Perhaps the answer lies in a sophisticated computer model.

There is No Consensus

The IPCC, the Obama administration, environmentalists, and most liberal politicians are all claiming a "consensus" on man-made climate change. They base this consensus on the most recent climate assessment report issued by the Intergovernmental Panel on Climate Change (IPCC), and a study entitled "Quantifying the Consensus on anthropogenic Global Warning in the Scientific Literature" by John Cook, published in 2013. With regard to the IPCC report, Professor Bob Carter, Chief Science Advisor of the International Climate Science Coalition immediately responded, "No one should trust the U.N. Intergovernmental Panel on Climate Change report issued today. The IPCC has a history of malfeasance that even includes rewording recommendations of expert science advisors to fit the alarmist agenda of participating governments." Australian climate analyst John McLean stated, "In previous IPCC assessment reports, media were tricked into reporting that thousands of climate experts endorsed the chapter in which climate change causes were discussed. In fact, only a few dozen scientists even commented on that part of the document." He concluded, saying "reporters should insist the IPCC reveal how many climate experts actually reviewed and agreed with each of AR5's most important conclusions."

Former climatology professor, Dr. Tim Ball, stated, "The IPCC's reputation is now beyond retrieval."

During the IPCC's prior assessment report (2007), only four of the twenty-three independent reviewers explicitly endorsed the chapter blaming humans for warming over the past fifty years. That's *not* a consensus.

The John Cook study was equally deceptive. Investigative reporters at *Popular Technology* concluded that the study, which claimed a ninety-seven percent consensus, falsely classified scientists' papers, according to confirmations from the scientists themselves. Their examination of the Cook study found that out of nearly 12,000 scientific papers that Cook's team evaluated, only sixty-five endorsed Cook's alarmist position. The ninety-seven percent consensus was later shown to be ninety-seven percent of the authors of those papers who expressed an opinion, which was only a fraction of the total. John Cook has refused to provide complete data on his study to the reporters, and has threatened legal action against anyone who discloses the full content. No consensus there, either.

In 1992, a petition was circulated by scientists informing the world of the false global warming narrative being portrayed by politicians and the media. It was signed by more than 4,000 scientists from 106 countries, including seventy-two Nobel Prize Winners. If factual scientific data had been reported by the media at that time, the subject of man-made global warming would not exist today.

Prior to the Kyoto Conference in 1997, a similar petition was signed by more than 15,000 scientists, most with advanced degrees, urging the U.S. Government to reject the Kyoto treaty. The scientists stated that the treaty was based on flawed ideas and was contrary to their research, which showed that actual atmospheric data did not support the climate models (IPCC) being cited by the United Nations and other promoters of the accord. Definitely, no consensus there.

In 2004, the Russian Academy of Sciences published a report concluding that the Kyoto Protocol has no scientific grounding at all.

Nobel Prize winning physicist Ivan Giaever resigned from the American Physical Society over their position that evidence for global warming was "incontrovertible." A subsequent editorial in the *Wall Street Journal*, signed by sixteen prominent scientists, supported Giaever's position and sharply criticized the "incontrovertible" claim.

In 2010, Marc Morano, Founder of ClimateDepot.com, released a list of more than 1000 scientists who challenged man-made global warming claims. The NIPCC also aggregated thousands of peer-reviewed scientific journal articles that do not support man-made climate change.

In May, 2012, the Heartland Institute held its 7th Annual International Conference on Climate Change. Approximately sixty scientists and policy experts discussed the causes and consequences of climate change, all of which supported the evidence that climate change is not human-caused. Thirty anthropogenic global warming scientists and alarmists were invited to explain and defend their scientific evidence. None showed up. Consensus?

And then, just when you thought it couldn't get any worse for the consensus-crowd, along came Greenpeace co-founder Patrick Moore, who testified before the Senate Environmental and Public Works Committee, Subcommittee on Oversight, regarding global warming. During his testimony, Mr. Moore stated, "There is no scientific proof that human emissions of carbon dioxide are the dominant cause of the minor warming of the earth's atmosphere over the past 100 years." He also claimed the IPCC's probability figures for man-made global warming had been invented, and that the IPCCs reliance on computer models was futile. Moore says he left Greenpeace after fifteen years when Greenpeace became more interested in politics than the environment.

In an interview with talk show host Sean Hannity, Mr. Moore stated, "CO2 is lower now than it has been through most of the history of life on earth, and so is the temperature." He concluded that "ice and frost are actually the enemies of life", not warming.

In early 2014, Germany and the EU started backing away from previously announced goals on reduction of carbon emissions.

These are just a few examples of instances that refute the claim of a consensus on man-made climate change. The media has been conditioned to accept the deception without question. You be the judge.

The IPCC

The Intergovernmental Panel on Climate Change (IPCC) was formed by the United Nations Environmental Programme (UNEP) and the World Meteorological Organization (WMO) in 1987. The stated goal of the IPCC was "To assess the available scientific, technical, and socio-economic information in the field of climate change."

Policy makers and the mainstream media view the IPCC reports as the "final word" on climate change and often use the report as the basis for critical decisions with regard to energy policy, which ultimately affects energy prices and regulations. I find this to be an extremely disturbing precedent because the IPCC is a political body, not a scientific body. Furthermore, the IPCC has had a questionable history ever since the release of its first climate report in 1990.

Virtually all of the IPCC's projections of future climate change are based on estimates using complex computer simulations called general circulation models (GCMs). These climate models exaggerate the likely outcome of global warming by displaying excessive sensitivity to carbon dioxide. In other words, the reports have consistently used inappropriate data and statistical basis, which made global warming appear worse via their method of assigning high values of climate sensitivity.

The IPCC was founded to find evidence of "human caused climate change", and as such, any research that could not be shown to support the pre-determined conclusion of a significant human fingerprint was largely dismissed. Despite their claims, the IPCC has never been able to demonstrate that climate change is significantly impacted by human activity. As each of the IPCC reports has been debunked, their supporting "evidence" has shifted dramatically from one false narrative to another. If climate science is "settled", as they claim, why does the IPCC's evidence of anthropogenic (human-caused) global warming keep changing over time? And why is so much observational and climatological data ignored or altered?

The first IPCC report (1990) used an improbable statistical method to suggest that warming in the early part of the twentieth century was due to human-produced greenhouse gases. No one believes this today.

The IPCC's second report (1995) invented the so-called "hot spot", a region showing an increased warming trend, with a maximum temperature in the equatorial troposphere. That evidence also disappeared, and a detailed analysis published in *Nature* (1996) showed that the hot spot never even existed.

That report, like all others, had been peer-reviewed. In other words, it had been read, discussed, modified, and approved by an international body of climate experts. However, the report released was not the report the contributing scientists approved. The report had been altered to remove statements critical of claims of man-made warming and greenhouse gas effects. In the chapter of the report that provided scientific evidence for and against a human influence over climate, fifteen sections were changed or deleted *after* scientists had signed off on the final draft. The following are three examples of statements that were deleted:

"None of the studies cited above has shown clear evidence that we can attribute the observed [climate] changes to the specific cause of increases in greenhouse gases."

"No study to-date has positively attributed all or part [of the climate observed to-date] to anthropogenic [man-made] causes."

"Any claims of positive detection of significant climate change are likely to remain controversial until uncertainties in the total natural variability of the climate system are reduced."

The obvious intent was to deceive policymakers and the public into believing scientific evidence supports the theory of human-caused global warming, and to provide cover for future political action.

When questioned about the deletions, the IPCC officials stated this was done "to ensure that it conformed to a 'policy maker's summary' of the full report." Interesting. Usually, a summary conforms to the underlying scientific data, rather than vice versa.

The IPCC's third report (2001), after two failed attempts to establish some kind of evidence for man-made global warming, adopted the infamous hockey-stick graph, which claimed that only the twentieth century showed unusual warming during the past 1000 years. That "evidence" was also proven to be manufactured and based on fictitious data (the Medieval Warm Period and Little Ice Age were omitted), erroneous statistical methods, and an inappropriate calibration method. The IPCC has since abandoned the hockey-stick graph.

When the IPCC released its fourth report in 2007, it won a share of the Nobel Peace Prize, along with Al Gore, "for their efforts to build up and disseminate greater knowledge about man-man climate change, and to lay the foundation for measures that are needed to counteract such change." Apparently the Nobel Foundation's nominating committee has no one who is science literate. Of the twenty-three independent reviewers of the IPCC's Fourth Assessment Report summary for policymakers, only four explicitly endorsed the key chapter blaming mankind for global warming over the past fifty years.

Not one of the climate models used in the IPCC's first four reports predicted the current eighteen-year temperature pause and virtually all models have shown modeling contrary to the actual temperatures over the last thirty-five years.

In its latest report (2013), the IPCC abandons all previous "evidence" and instead concentrates on trying to prove that the reported surface warming between 1978 and 2000 agrees with warming predicted by the climate models. However, the reported warming only applies to land-based weather stations and is not seen in any other data. The weather-satellite data shows no significant changes in atmospheric temperatures. Neither does proxy data (analysis of tree rings, ocean/lake sediments, stalagmites, etc.). Since the temperature data cited by the IPCC is only found in land-based weather stations, it is possible the placement of the weather stations could be impacting temperature data due to the Urban Heat Island (UHI) effect, which I discuss later in this chapter.

What was acknowledged in the latest IPCC report is that nearly all of the computer models have been wrong, and the hockey-stick graph used in the past was not accurate and has been abandoned. They also admitted there have been no increases in droughts, hurricanes, typhoons, and other forms of extreme weather, and they concede for the first time that global temperatures have not risen since 1998.

In February, 2014, the Global Warming Policy Foundation (GWPF) released its review of the IPCC's 2013 climate report. The GWPF found that IPCC's report failed to provide an adequate assessment of climate sensitivity, both in ECS (equilibrium climate sensitivity) and TCR (transient climate response), which are the most important parameters in the climate discussion. Actual ECS data indicates that the rate of climate change will be much less than that indicated in the IPCC report. This is an extremely important revelation. If the IPCC report had provided accurate information, the urgency of global warming would have disappeared. The newest research by GWPF indicates an ECS value that is less than 2°C, well below the ECS of 4.5°C which the IPCC had indicated as "likely."

The GWPF report confirms that the IPCC report confused readers with evidence that was outdated, already disproven, based on assumptions, not directly applicable, or totally false. The IPCC reports are also written so that many parts are not easily understood by policymakers, in areas of the report such as those addressing complexity and behavior of climate sensitivity. Ultimately, the policy makers and the public have been misled.

There have been numerous examples of policies being implemented based on so-called evidence provided by the IPCC. A prime example is the Kyoto Protocol, an international treaty adopted in December of 1997, aimed at reducing the emissions of greenhouse gases that contribute to global warming. In force since 2005, the protocol called for reducing the emissions of six greenhouse gases in forty-one countries, plus the European Union, to 5.2 percent below 1990 levels during the commitment period of 2008-2012. Assuming that all commitments will be met, the Kyoto Protocol will end up costing trillions of dollars, but deliver no significant cooling (less than .02°C by 2050).

At the time of the Kyoto Conference, a petition was signed by more than 15,000 scientists, most with advanced degrees, urging the U.S. Government to reject the treaty. The scientists stated that the treaty was based on flawed ideas and was contrary to their research, which showed that actual atmospheric data did not support the climate models being cited by the United Nations and other promoters of the accord. The number of scientists voting against this treaty indicates that most scientists are frustrated about the misuse of science, especially inaccurate science, to promote a political agenda that sees billions of dollars being spent on the imaginary consequences of global warming while other valid fields of science, such as medical and agricultural research are losing research money. With this many scientists openly critical of the IPCC reports even back then, the claim of an anthropogenic climate change consensus is, it seems, obviously total fiction.

The IPCC theory is driven by just a handful of scientists and favorable reviewers, not the 2500-4000 usually cited. The Absurd Claims of the IPCC are now being offset by the fact-based publications of the Nongovernmental International Panel on Climate Change (NIPCC).

NIPCC

The Nongovernmental International Panel on Climate Change (NIPCC) was formed in 2008 by an independent team of scientists with no political agenda. Their mission has simply been to provide factual information with regard to climate science. The NIPCC uses the same peer-reviewed science as the IPCC, however they base their findings on all available research, including instrumental observations. The IPCC findings are based on climate models—which can be easily manipulated—and have proven to be highly inaccurate.

The NIPCC charter is to investigate causes and consequences of climate change from all perspectives, not just from human influence.

Based upon all available data, the NIPCC has reached an entirely different set of conclusions than the IPCC. The NIPCC scientists have found no concrete evidence that supports a dangerous warming trend. They have also found that climate changes are due to natural causes alone.

The latest NIPCC report, titled Climate Change Reconsidered II: Physical Science, concludes that "neither the rate nor the magnitude of the reported late twentieth century surface warming (1979 to 2000) lies outside normal natural variability, nor is it in any way unusual compared to earlier episodes in earth's history."

The report also concludes that no unambiguous evidence exists for adverse changes to the global environment caused by human-related CO2 emission, and that future warming, if any, due to human greenhouse gases, is not likely to exceed one to two degrees Celsius. The report also finds that higher levels of carbon dioxide will not cause extreme weather, melting ice caps, or rising sea levels.

In its review of the latest IPCC report (September, 2013), the NIPCC challenged the IPCC's claim of a ninety-five percent certainty that there is man-made global warming. The NIPCC found that the ninety-five percent certainty was based solely on a limited number of climate models that agreed with each other on man-made global warming, not actual observations. The actual observations show no indication of human influence on global warming. In other words, they (IPCC) are using models that match their narrative, rather than allowing the narrative to match the facts.

The NIPCC concluded, "The current generation of global climate models is unable to make accurate projections of climate even ten years ahead, let alone the 100-year period that has been adopted by policy planners. The output of such models should therefore not be used to guide public policy formulation until they have been validated and shown to have predictive value."

The emergence of the NIPCC as a more viable and reputable source of factual climate information has forced the IPCC to retreat from at least eleven of its earlier claims. Even so, the IPCC's latest report is still far from accurate.

As the NIPCC continues to gain popularity, the IPCC will either have to change its entire narrative on man-made climate change, or eventually lose what little credibility it has left.

Carbon Dioxide

Since carbon dioxide (CO_2) is professed to be the primary villain in the global warming saga, perhaps a brief tutorial on CO_2 is in order.

The central premise of the alarmist global warming theory is that carbon dioxide emissions should be directly and indirectly trapping a certain amount of heat in the earth's atmosphere and preventing it from escaping into space (the Greenhouse Effect). What they fail to mention is that CO_2 is a "trace gas" in the atmosphere and is measured in parts per million (ppm). Carbon dioxide accounts for less than .0004 (4 ten-thousandths of one percent) of the earth's atmosphere, and only about three percent of that is produced by human activity. The total of manmade CO_2 emissions throughout human history account for less that 0.00022 percent of the total naturally emitted from the mantle of the earth during geological history. Two-hundred-million years ago, when dinosaurs roamed the earth, carbon dioxide concentration in the atmosphere was 1800 ppm—five times higher than today. The result was lush tropical forests virtually from pole to pole.

As we learned in our high school science classes, carbon dioxide is needed by plants for the process of photosynthesis to occur. The only proven effect of rising carbon dioxide in the atmosphere is an increase in plant growth. Actually, rising CO_2 levels may be our best hope of increasing crop yields to feed the ever-growing world population. A composite of 279 research studies predicts that overall plant growth rates will ultimately double as carbon dioxide increases. Standing timber in the U.S. hardwood forests has doubled in the last fifty years. Thousands of studies have shown that increases in CO_2 produce better fruits, vegetables, trees, and most other forms of plant life. Cereal crops do especially well.

Another aspect of carbon dioxide that needs to be understood is its contribution as a greenhouse gas. The most abundant greenhouse gas is water vapor, which accounts for ninety-five percent of the greenhouse effects. The remaining five percent is made up of CO_2, methane, nitrous oxide, and minute portions of numerous other gases. When water vapor is included, the human-caused CO_2 footprint is reduced to .117% of the greenhouse effect. Yes, one hundred seventeen thousandths of one percent!

Water vapor is the key to understanding the impact of carbon dioxide increase on climate. The climate models the alarmists refer to assume that an increase in water vapor as the earth's climate warms will magnify the effect of the carbon dioxide, when , in fact, increased water vapor may actually reduce the effect of carbon dioxide. Even without the impact of water vapor, an increase in CO_2 in the atmosphere has minimal effect because it only absorbs certain wave lengths of radiant energy. As radiation in a particular wave length band is used up, it leaves less available for absorption. Consider, too, that CO_2 is not even the most efficient greenhouse gas for retaining heat from the sun. Methane is twenty-one times more effective at heat retention, and nitrous oxide is 310 times more effective. Collectively, they still have very little impact.

The single most important thing you need to know about CO_2 in the global warming discussion is this: carbon dioxide levels increase and decrease as a result of temperature variances. Nine-hundred-thousand years of ice-core-temperature records and CO_2 content records show that carbon dioxide increases follow increases in earth temperature, which is logical since oceans are the primary source of carbon dioxide. As the global climate cools, the oceans absorb more carbon dioxide. As the climate warms, the oceans release carbon dioxide. Thus, the alarmist claims that increasing CO_2 levels *cause* global warming is totally false. Increased CO_2 is the *result* of warming temperatures.

It appears more likely that climate change is controlled by variations in solar magnetic activity and by periodic changes in ocean circulation. During the current 300-year recovery period from the Little Ice Age, temperature variations have correlated almost perfectly with fluctuations in solar activity. This correlation long predates the start of the industrial period.

The bottom line is this: The amount of man-made carbon dioxide in the atmosphere is insignificant. The oceans are the biggest source of CO_2 by far. Decomposing vegetation is also a huge contributor. But man . . . not so much. Carbon dioxide levels throughout history were many times higher than they are now, without causing runaway global warming. Higher levels of carbon dioxide have proven to be beneficial, as previously mentioned.

Climate Models

Almost all of the IPCC's projections of future climate change are based on computer model simulations which, as explained previously, are known as general circulation models (GCMs). The problem with climate models is that they've all been wrong, and will likely continue to be wrong in the future. Global climate models can only produce meaningful results if we already know exactly how the global climate works, which we do not. They are not designed to produce predictions of future climate, only "what if" scenarios based on arbitrarily selected variables. The results can change dramatically when even a few of the variables are changed, and as we've seen with the IPCC reports, the data can be manipulated to arrive at a pre-determined conclusion. Climate models are simply computerized forecasting aids, not evidence. Experts in computer modeling agree that no current climate model has been capable of making accurate predictions of a regional climate change, even when all measured data inputs were known and available. This is because climate models omit important factors such as changes in ocean currents or solar magnetic activity, and our knowledge of the relevant physics is far from complete. Most climate models display too much sensitivity to carbon dioxide concentrations and in almost all cases exaggerate the likely path of global warming. Good empirical estimates of long-term warming show expectations of future warming will be at least forty to fify percent lower than predicted by the climate models. Climate models attempt to simulate cloud action over decades, which is impossible. Global weather is so complicated that it is difficult to predict cloud behavior for even a week. This factor alone renders the climate model estimates virtually useless.

Some computer models have predicted the average global temperature will increase by as much as 60°C over the next hundred years, while other models have predicted significant cooling over the same period, so you can see the ambiguity inherent in all predictions.

Howard Hayden PH.D., Professor of Physics at the University of Connecticut, recently stated, "If the science were as certain as climate activists pretend, then there would be precisely one climate model, and it would be in agreement with measured data. As it happens, climate modelers have constructed literally dozens of climate models. What they all have in common is a failure to agree with the other climate models."

Another glaring problem with most computer models is that they claim increases in carbon dioxide levels are the cause of global warming, when in fact empirical data has shown that it is warming that historically causes an increase of CO2, once again rendering the climate models useless. Patrick Moore, co-founder of Greenpeace, stated, "You could learn more about the future by throwing a bunch of bones on the ground than you could by a lot of these climate models . . . they are not something you can predict the future of the earth with."

Still, government climate policies are all being based on the estimates of these models, and the latest IPCC report claims a ninety-five percent certainty that global warming is human-caused. Their explanation is that ninety-five percent of the climate models agree. Therefore, the actual observations must be wrong. Or could it be that ninety-five percent of the climate models used in this limited sampling were calibrated to arrive at a pre-determined conclusion? As Professor Chris Folland from the Hadley Centre for Climate Prediction and Research once stated, "The data doesn't matter. We're not basing our recommendations on the data. We're basing them on the climate models." That, my friends, is what we're up against.

The Urban Heat Island Effect

Earlier in this chapter, I mentioned the Urban Heat Island effect with regard to location of land-based weather stations. This is significant in the discussion of global warming and deserves a more complete examination.

Much of the evidence used to support the claim of man-made global warming is based on surface temperature data. This data is collected by numerous land-based weather stations around the world and subsequently used by climate models to predict future temperature trends. There are several problems with using this type of data as a prediction method.

First, seventy-one percent of the earth's surface is covered with water, so land-based weather stations only provide relevant data from 29 percent of the earth.

Secondly, as Professor John Christy, University of Huntsville Alabama stated, "If you want to know how the climate system works, you should look at the bulk of the atmosphere, and pay less attention to the surface thermometers."

Why? Because, surface temperature readings can be unreliable. One cause of unreliable readings is the Urban Heat Island (UHI)

Effect. As the name implies, UHI refers to the tendency of an urban area to remain warmer than the surrounding area, by as much as 10 degrees, due to a lack of vegetation and soil moisture, plus the heat absorption and retention of man-made structures (Concrete, asphalt, metal, etc.) Many weather stations are located in areas considered to be Urban Heat Islands. An example of the impact can be found in a recent study published in Theoretical and Applied Climatology.

The study examined daily temperature readings from five weather stations in North China, one urban and four rural, over a period of 50 years. They found that the trends of annual extreme temperatures were significantly different between the urban and rural stations. 100 percent of the reported artificial trends in the number of hot days and 94.1 percent of the artificial trend in extreme maximum temperatures were due to the poor location of the stations, and had nothing to do with alleged man-made global warming.

Given that seventy-one percent of the earth is ocean, and the bulk of the climate changes have atmospheric origins, how can we possibly rely on climate models that are created using this type of data?

A Tale of Two Scandals

Aside from being an overall hoax, climate hysteria has spawned its share of scandals. I will discuss two of them. One, Climategate, you may have heard of. The other, Wikipedia, you probably haven't heard about. Both are equally disturbing.

The Climategate scandal uncovered an extensive public campaign of misinformation regarding global warming and the denigration of scientists who did not believe carbon dioxide emissions caused climate change.

In November, 2009, hackers uncovered hundreds of emails at the U.K.'s University of East Anglia exposing private conversations among top-level British and U.S. climate scientists. The emails discussed whether certain data should be released to the public, and also referred to statistical tricks that had been used to manufacture climate trends and distort climate models to show a recent spike in global warming, which was non-existent. The data had been deliberately modified to reach a preconceived conclusion. One example was the infamous hockey-stick graph. The group also made unethical attempts to suppress contrary findings and pressure scientific publications from printing articles that disagreed with the narrative of man-made warming. Former Vice-President Al Gore relied heavily on the altered hockey-stick graph as evidence of human-caused global warming in his documentary *An Inconvenient Truth*. The data was also used by the IPCC in their third assessment report, which has since been debunked.

The Climategate emails exposed the fact that the peer-review process, once considered the gold standard for vetting scientific publications, was subject to manipulation.

The Wikipedia scandal is even more disturbing. Beginning in 2003, a Green Party activist named William Connolley was granted a senior editorial and administrative status at Wikipedia, the most used information source in the world, and the third most popular non-search engine site on the web. Connelly immediately began to rewrite articles on climate change, the greenhouse effect, instrumental temperature data, climate models, global cooling, etc. He also rewrote articles on the politics of global warming, the Medieval Warm Period, and the Little Ice Age. Articles Connelly disagreed with were either rewritten or removed completely. Wikipedia, by virtue of its decentralized format makes it difficult to combat concerted efforts to maliciously alter its content and Connelly, as a website administrator, was able to act with virtual impunity.

Wikipedia articles that debunked or offered evidence contrary to the IPCC reports and climate models were either "scrubbed" or deleted.

Over a six-and-a-half year period, Connolley rewrote or created 5,428 Wikipedia articles. He removed over 500 articles, and barred over 2000 contributors whose views ran contrary to his. The articles in Wikipedia dealing with climate change became nothing more than Left-wing misinformation.

In September, 2009, the Wikipedia Arbitration Committee revoked Connolley's administrator status, which did little to improve Wikipedia's "slant" on climate reporting. Even today, Wikipedia sites pertaining to climate change are heavily biased in favor of the belief of man-made global warming, despite overwhelming evidence to the contrary. Even in the articles titled "Global Warming Controversy" and "Global Warming Denial", evidence contrary to anthropogenic global warming is not even displayed. It would appear Wikipedia has no intention of maintaining a politically neutral position.

I recently went to Wikipedia and looked up William Connolley. Let's just say that the article appears to have been "massaged" to reflect a more positive image. It also appears that William Connolley may have been the masseuse.

In Their Own Words

There *is* no consensus on man-made climate change. There are far more scientists who dispute the claim of human-caused climate change than those who support it. The following are merely a sampling of comments made by climate scientists and others directly related to the field of climate science, many of whom were involved with at least one or more of the IPCC's climate reports.

> "Worst scientific scandal in history . . . when people come to know what the truth is, they will feel deceived by science and scientists." UN IPCC Scientist Dr. Kiminori Itoh, Award-Winning PHD Environmental Physical Chemist

"The whole climate change issue is about to fall apart—heads will roll." South African U.N. Scientist Dr. Will Alexander

"The claims of the IPCC are dangerous unscientific nonsense." Dr. Vincent Gray , IPCC reviewer and climate researcher

"Gore prompted me to start delving into the science (man-made global warming) again and I quickly found myself solidly in the skeptic camp." Meteorologist Hajo Smit, Former member of Dutch UN IPCC Committee

"It doesn't matter what is true, it only matters what people believe is true." Prof. **Chris Folland, Hadley Centre** for Climate Prediction and Research

"I personally cannot in good faith continue to contribute to a process that I view as both being motivated by pre-conceived agendas and being scientifically unsound." Christopher W. Landsea, Former IPCC author and reviewer

"The idea that climate change poses an existential threat to humankind is laughable." UN IPCC lead author, Dr. Richard Tol

"[Those who] seem to naively believe that the climate change science espoused in the [U.N's] Intergovernmental Panel on Climate Change (IPCC) documents represents 'scientific consensus.' Nothing could be further from the truth." Dr. Madhav Khandekar, UN IPCC Scientist

"Here was a purely political body posing as a scientific institution." Dr. John Brignell, Engineering Professor University of South Hampton referring to IPCC

"Such hysteria [over global warming] simply represents the scientific illiteracy of much of the public, [and] the susceptibility of the public to the substitution of repetition for truth." Richard Lindzen, Professor of Atmospheric Sciences, MIT

"Temperature measurements show that the [climate model-predicted mid-troposphere] hot zone is non-existent. This is more than sufficient to invalidate global climate models and projections made with them." UN IPCC Scientist Dr. Steven M. Japar, PhD, Atmospheric Chemist

"The warming we have had in the last 100 years is so small that if we didn't have climatologists to measure it we wouldn't have noticed at all." Dr. Lennart Bengtsson, Former UN IPCC climate scientist

"The Kyoto [global warming] theorists have put the cart before the horse. It is global warming that triggers higher levels of carbon dioxide in the atmosphere, not the other way around." Andrei Kapitsa, Russian geographer and Antarctic ice core researcher

"My own belief concerning anthropogenic [man-made] climate change is that models do not realistically simulate the climate system because there are many very important sub-grid scale processes that the models either replicate poorly or completely omit . . . Some scientists have manipulated the observed data to justify their model results . . . There is no rational justification for using climate model forecasts to determine public policy." John S. Theon, retired Chief of NASA's Climate Processes Research Program

"No matter if the science of global warming is all phony . . . climate change [provides] the greatest opportunity to bring about justice and equality in the world." Christine Stewart, Canadian Minister of the Environment

". . .we need to get some broad based support, to capture the public's imagination. That, of course, entails getting loads of media coverage. So we have to offer up scary scenarios, make simplified dramatic statements, and make little mention of the doubts we might have. Each of us has to decide what the right balance is between being effective and being honest." Professor Stephen Schneider, IPCC lead author

"The great climate science centers around the world are more than well aware how weak their science is."

"The problem is we don't know what the climate is doing. We thought we knew 20 years ago."

"Something like 80% of the measurements being made during that time were either faked or incompetently done."

"IPCC is too politicized and too internalized." —James Lovelock, Geophysicist and Environmentalist

"We can expect climate crisis industry to grow increasingly shrill, and increasingly hostile toward anyone who questions their authority." Dr. Kenneth Green, Environmental Scientist and UN IPCC Reviewer

Just as Dr. Green had anticipated, the climate alarmists have grown increasingly hostile as more and more evidence debunking their science is revealed.

Unfortunately, even as the majority of people become educated to the facts of true climate science, there will always be a core group of alarmists whose financial or political agendas get in the way of common sense.

Follow the Money

In reference to the issue of climate alarmism, German economist Ottmar Edenhoffer stated, "this has almost nothing to do with environmental policy . . . one must say clearly that we redistribute de facto the world's wealth by climate policy . . . One has to free oneself from the illusion that international climate policy is environmental policy. This has almost nothing to do with environmental policy anymore."

Edenhoffer was right. In the United States alone, billions of dollars are taken each year from unknowing U.S. taxpayers and spent on a mythical problem that only exists in contrived climate models. Some estimates put the spending at one billion dollars per day. Carbon-based energy, the lifeblood of the world's economy, is slowly giving way to "green" energy. Those who control the prevailing energy sources control the respective economies. Environmental causes provide a convenient conduit for the expansion of governmental overreach.

Global warming alarmism offers an excuse for governments to increase taxes and create taxpayer-funded green energy projects. The greater the fear of a climate catastrophe, the more amenable people will be to accepting higher taxes and higher energy costs. The increase in energy costs will affect those in the lower income brackets particularly hard, and many will be forced to rely on energy vouchers or other assistance to pay their bills. The result will be yet another segment of the population which has become dependent on the government.

In the U.S. there are currently eighteen federal agencies engaged in activities related to global warming. Hundreds of thousands of jobs have been created within government, the science community, and the media as a result of the myth of man-made climate change. Those who express belief in human-caused global warming are much more likely to get research grants and better positions than those who express doubt. Expressing doubt as a scientist could end research funding and be a career killer. As such, those in the green energy field tend to espouse a liberal mindset, at least publicly.

Tom Steyer, Democrat billionaire and founder of Farallon Capital Management, is donating tens of millions of dollars to further the narrative of man-made global warming. Is it being done to protect the environment? That's doubtful. Steyer has made a fortune in oil investments. However, a small number of ultra-rich Democrats like Steyer and Al Gore stand to make billions of dollars from green-energy investments. They appear to use their wealth and connections to purchase government decisions which will advance their own personal interests.

In Nevada, Senator Harry Reid has also done well with regard to green energy projects. Three of Reid's pet projects, Nevada Geothermal, Ormat Nevada, and Solar Reserve received a combined $1.18 billion in loans between September, 2010 and September, 2011. All of the money came from the SWIP-E project, which Reid campaigned on. Executives of those three companies have donated huge sums of money to Reid and other Democrat campaigns since 2008.

In August, 2010, Bright Source Energy (a solar project) hosted a fundraiser for Senator Reid in its Oakland offices. Eight months later, Bright Source Energy was awarded a $1.6 billion loan guarantee from the Department of Energy. Bernie Toon, former Chief of Staff to then Senator Joe Biden, was also hired by Bright Source and paid $40,000.00 to lobby on their behalf.

Virtually all of the Energy Department's loan portfolio has gone to individuals or companies with extensive ties to democrat politicians, either top donors, fundraisers, or campaign contribution bundlers.

In March, 2014, Senator James Inhofe (R- Okla.), stated during the Defense Department's fiscal year 2015 budget hearing, that President Obama had wasted $120 billion on global warming over the past five years.

$120 billion is more than twice the annual Social Security deficit.

Conclusion

There is no definitive scientific evidence that human-caused release of carbon dioxide, methane, or any other greenhouse gas will result in catastrophic global warming or other climate anomalies. There is no compelling proof to support any degree of man-made climate change. As such, calls for immediate action to mitigate the threat of climate disasters through de-carbonization of the world, are baseless and irresponsible. A handful of IPCC scientists, environmentalists, green-energy investors, and the media are all complicit in the promotion of the man-made climate change hoax.

Policymakers have not been given reliable and accurate information with regard to climate science. If they had, this issue would have been dropped twenty years ago. Unfortunately, climate science is being contaminated by political agendas. Every political candidate should support rational measures to protect and improve the environment, but it does not make sense to back expensive programs that divert resources from proven needs. Scientists are concerned when they see billions of dollars per year devoted to research based on the imaginary consequences of a hypothetical problem, while other fields of science are starving.

We need to take a rational scientific approach, not an emotional approach, to the study of climate change within the context of known natural climate history. We know that climate models, the basis for the IPCC reports, are not accurate and may never be accurate, simply due to the thousands of variables that come into play and the potential for manipulation.

Yet those of us who provide sound, factual climate data are met with bullying tactics and name-calling by leftist politicians and the media. The climate alarmists accuse us of being totally ignorant of climate science. In reality, it is they who are either ignorant or have simply chosen to ignore it. Once you cut through the rhetoric and name-calling, all the alarmists have to support their position is a movie made by an out-of-touch politician and climate models based on theoretical scenarios.

In contrast, there are mountains of solid data available that effortlessly debunk the myth of human-caused climate change. As the so-called "evidence" for man-made climate change evaporates, solutions for dealing with natural climate variances are becoming increasingly clear. Rather than trying to mitigate a threat that will likely never happen, governments are turning more frequently to adaptation, a far less expensive alternative. At present, the costs of reducing carbon emissions vastly exceed the benefits. The annual cost per U.S. household is estimated at $3900.00, and there would be extensive job loss if full measures that are currently recommended are taken.

If it became evident to everyone that the earth is not facing a climatological apocalypse, we could save lots of money. Plus, if the media played their cards right, the disappearance of this hoax could provide them an opportunity to regain a little credibility . . . but not much.

We cannot, as a country, continue to accept the lies, the fear-mongering, and the bullying tactics that continue to drive up our cost of living and diminish our quality of life. This chapter has given you the ammo to fight and win the conversation on climate change. Do not remain silent any longer.

Please, continue to do your research. Be a critical thinker. The facts on climate change are sometimes hard to find, but you owe it to yourself to find them.

CHAPTER THREE

The Race Card

For years, conservatives have sat back and allowed the media and the Democratic Party to perpetuate a false narrative with regard to racism. For too long, many Americans, ignorant of history, have bought into the claim of conservative racism. And the conservatives have done a poor job of articulating their defense.

In both principle and practice, the Republican Party has a far better track record than the Democrats when it comes to race. On issues that affect African-Americans, Democratic Party policies have continued to have a negative impact. The ease with which the Democrats have played the African-American community is frightening. The black community is now asking what fifty years of support for the Democratic Party has gotten them. The answer is more government dependency, a lower standard of living, and a party more interested in retaining power than helping their own people.

The Democratic Party has done nothing for the black community beyond a never-ending cycle of social-welfare programs that provide no escape. The programs of the Great Society failed to achieve their stated goal and the social conditions of the African-Americans actually became worse. But, success was never really the intended outcome. The hidden goal of the Great Society programs was to create dependency and a perpetual voting block. Without the black vote, the Democrats would lose. So it has been in the best interest of the Democrats to maintain or increase the level of government dependency.

The same is true with regard to racism. Without divisive issues such as racism, Democrats would have to convince the African-American community to vote for them based on their platform, which has ideals contrary to those of the majority of blacks, or Americans of any race. Today's charges of racism have little to do with race, but everything to do with politics.

African-Americans would be wise to assess the value and substance of all political parties, and, hopefully, once they examine facts, become part of a larger demographic that sees increasing employment and educational opportunities. They need to see for themselves that true racism is relatively scarce, once they distance themselves from the "civil rights leaders" and the liberal media, who try to convince them they are victims, devoid of the opportunity for a better life.

Martin Luther King once stated, "We must learn to live together as brothers or perish together as fools." Living together as brothers means we must create and maintain an open, honest dialog, free of the constraints of political correctness and racial overtones. Discussions concerning valid social issues are often suppressed in the name of political correctness, at the expense of those they would supposedly offend.

In 1965, Democrat Senator Daniel Patrick Moynihan released a report called "The Negro Family: The Case for National Action." It is considered one of the most relevant social commentaries ever written with regard to the struggles of the African-American community. The report has proven to be accurate in its predictions, yet Moynihan was labeled a racist for daring to write about matters of the black community. Had the content of the report been assimilated, rather than perceived with racist intent, some of the subsequent problems within the African-American community may have been avoided.

As a result of situations like this, the American public has gone overboard on political correctness. Today, people would rather ignore the issues than risk being labeled racists, regardless of who is suffering or what the cost.

It has taken decades of tragedy for society to admit there is something seriously wrong in the black community, particularly in the inner cities.

While paying them lip service, Democrats have passed legislation, such as a broken welfare system, that rewards poor mothers for having children out-of-wedlock and punishes them for being married. In 1965, over seventy-six percent of black children were born to married women. Today, seventy-three percent of black children are born out of wedlock, and sixty-seven percent live in single-parent homes.

Prior to the programs of the Great Society, black teenage pregnancies had been decreasing, poverty and dependency were declining, and income among blacks was increasing in both absolute and relative terms compared to white income. Prior to the 1960s, the unemployment rate for black teenagers was under ten percent. Today, black teen unemployment is almost forty percent. Since the 1970s, marriage in the African-American community is down by thirty-four percent—double the national average. The children, through no fault of their own, are often raised in environments without fathers, where there may be violence, drugs, poor educational opportunities, and government dependency.

Racism is the usual explanation for the decline of the African-American family, but that claim doesn't fly.

Most major American cities, like Detroit, Chicago, Washington D.C., and Los Angeles have been run by liberal Democrats for decades. These once great cities have been overrun with gangs, violence, drugs, and economic collapse. Yet they keep electing liberal Democrats and blaming the "racist" Republicans for their problems.

Malcolm X had it right when he stated, "White liberals who have been posing as our friends have failed us." Neither Malcolm X nor MLK would approve of the way African-Americans have become wards of the state.

History of Racism

There has been a lot of misinformation circulated over the years with regard to origins and beliefs of various political parties. Democrats claim Republicans are the party of racism, especially the more conservative elements of the Republican Party, such as the Tea Party. The Republicans make the same claim about the Democrats. So which, if either, is the party of racism? History paints a very clear picture; the answer may surprise you.

The Republican Party was founded primarily to oppose slavery, and Republicans who eventually abolished slavery. The Republicans also fought to grant equal rights and citizenship to the freed slaves. In 1865, the Thirteenth Amendment formally and legally freeing the slaves, was passed with every Republican in the House and Senate voting in favor. Less than one-quarter of the Democrats voted in favor of its passage. Then, despite strong Democratic opposition, Republicans passed the Fourteenth Amendment, which granted citizenship to former slaves, and the Fifteenth Amendment, which gave blacks the right to vote.

Nathan Bedford Forrest, a Democrat, founded the Ku Klux Klan as an extension of the Southern Democratic Party. The Klan's objective was to terrorize and suppress African-Americans and their supporters. Virtually all lynchings of blacks took place in regions controlled by Democrats.

Abraham Lincoln was a Republican. Unfortunately his vice-president, Andrew Johnson, was a Democrat. Johnson, along with the Southern Democrats, were against civil rights for the freed slaves and vigorously fought against them after Lincoln's assassination.

It was the Democratic Party that instituted the Jim Crow Laws, which made sure blacks would remain second-class citizens, even after the ratification of the Reconstruction Amendments, laws that provided "separate, but equal" status for African-Americans. The resulting separation, however, led to a number of disadvantages for the African-American community with regard to education, housing, social acceptance, and employment opportunities, to name a few.

During the Reconstruction Period, the Democrats also imposed a poll tax as a means of circumventing the Fifteenth Amendment and preventing large numbers of blacks from voting.

In 1936, after the Berlin Olympics, Democrat President Franklin D. Roosevelt invited the white American athletes to meet with him. The black athletes were not invited. President Roosevelt also implemented one of the most egregious racist policies of the 20th Century, the Japanese internment camps, during World War II.

It was Republican Dwight Eisenhower who pushed to pass the Civil Rights Act of 1957 and sent troops to Arkansas to desegregate the schools. The leading proponent of school segregation was Democrat Governor George Wallace. In Martin Luther King's "I have a dream" speech, it was Wallace who King was referring to when he said, "I have a dream that one day down in Alabama, with its vicious racists, with its governor having his lips dripping with the words of interposition and nullification . . ." In case you were wondering, Dr. Martin Luther King was a Republican.

It was Democrat President John F. Kennedy who had Dr. King wire-tapped and investigated by the FBI.

It was the Democrats who stood in the schoolhouse doors, and it was the Democrats who turned on the skin-burning fire hoses, and unleashed vicious dogs on the marchers in Birmingham.

Which brings us to the mid-1960s. This is the period when the Democrats, clearly the party of racism up to that point, claim the parties "switched" and the Republicans became the party of racism. So, how did that magically happen? And why did both parties maintain all other facets of their respective platforms? The fact is, they never did "switch." The Democrats simply changed from overt racism to a more veiled form of racism, disguised as government assistance programs, which like the belladonna flower, were pleasing to the eye, but came with serious side-effects.

On July 2, 1964, Congress enacted the Civil Rights Act of 1964. This legislation outlawed discrimination against minorities and women, including all forms of racial segregation. Although this Act was initiated by Democrat President John F. Kennedy, it was actually supported by a larger percentage of Republicans than Democrats in both the House and the Senate. In the House, eighty percent of the Republicans voted in favor of the Act, compared to sixty-three percent of the Democrats. The Senate vote was similar with eighty-two percent of Republicans and sixty-nine percent of Democrats voting in favor. Only four Senate Republicans voted against the Act, with twenty-one Democrats voting against it. The Democrats who voted against the Civil Rights Act included Robert Byrd (former KKK member), William Fulbright (Bill Clinton's mentor), and Al Gore, Sr.

Overall, there were twenty-six major civil rights votes from 1933 through the civil rights' period of the 1960s. The Republicans voted in favor of civil rights over ninety-five percent of the time. During that same period, Democrats voted *against* civil rights *eighty-percent* of the time.

At the time the Civil Rights Act was being debated, President Lyndon B. Johnson and the Democrats launched The Great Society, a set of domestic programs aimed at reducing poverty levels and curbing racial injustices. Although the Great Society was billed as the "cure all" for the social and economic ills of the time, there may have been an ulterior motive for creating those programs. The black voters had been a reliable Republican voting block for decades, and the Democrats wanted the African-

American vote. President Johnson was not shy about his belief that government dependency would secure the African-American vote. As he most eloquently stated in reference to the Great Society programs, "I'll have those niggers voting Democrat for the next 200 years." If I were African-American, that statement alone would have kept me solidly in the Republican camp, not just for the use of the word "nigger", but for the premeditated and calculated result he envisioned. Unfortunately, the media didn't give that statement any coverage. The result of the Great Society programs has been an ever-increasing base of people, many able-bodied working-age adults, from all races, who have become totally dependent on the government.

Since the Great Society, the African-American population has become a Democratic monolith. Since 1964, no Republican presidential candidate has received more than fifteen- percent of the black vote, despite the fact that only twenty-eight percent of black Americans consider themselves liberal. So, other than government dependency, what has fifty years supporting the Democratic Party gotten them? Blacks voided their traditional attachment to the party of Lincoln to become Democrats by virtue of economic expediency, not by principle, and now they are paying a heavy price.

Who has been representing the Democratic Party over the last fifty years? The first person who comes to mind is Senator Robert Byrd, who held office from 1959 to 2010. The former Ku Klux Klan member was referred to by his fellow Democrats as the "Conscience of The Senate." Keep in mind this is the man who once wrote, "I shall never fight in the armed forces with a Negro by my side . . . rather I should die a thousand times, and see Old Glory trampled in the dirt never to rise again, than to see this beloved land of ours become degraded by race mongrels." He also called Dr. Martin Luther King a "troublemaker" and a "coward."

The next name that comes to mind is Bill Clinton, who was sometimes sarcastically referred to as the "first black president." In 1989, then Governor Clinton was one of three Arkansas officials sued for intimidation of black voters under the 1965 Voting Rights Act. For years, Clinton belonged to a country club in Arkansas that excluded blacks from membership. Also, in a conversation about Barack Obama, Clinton was overheard saying, "A few years ago, this guy would have been carrying our bags." The Democrats consider Clinton to be the party flag-bearer. So, in all honesty, who is the Party of Racism?

In April, 2013, the National Urban League released its Annual State of Black America report. The report concluded that equality between black and white Americans has improved little since the Civil Rights Movement. So, let me ask you one more time. "What has voting for the Democrats gotten the African-American community over the last fifty years?"

The Media on Racism

The media has played a major role in the deterioration of race relations in America, especially in recent years. The reporting has become biased and disproportionate. Paula Deen was kicked off of her TV network for admitting she used a derogatory racial term a few decades ago, yet Alec Baldwin, Lee Daniels, and other members of the liberal Hollywood elite get a pass from the media when constantly using racial or homophobic slurs. Oprah Winfrey can concoct tales of victimization by a white shop girl, and Al Sharpton can create hate crimes where there were none, but a rodeo clown in Missouri is banned for life because he wore an Obama mask, and a filmmaker is jailed for simply making a film that exposed the truths of the Muslim religion.

The media sacrifices solid journalism for political correctness and a liberal agenda. Black personalities can use racist remarks with virtual impunity. During a live broadcast on C-SPAN in October, 2005, Kamau Kambon, a black professor, stated, "We have to exterminate white people off the face of the planet." During an interview with Bill O'Reilly, Quannell X, a black author and radio personality, stated, "I say in the words of Malcolm X, if you find any good white people, kill them now before they turn bad." There was no media outcry. What do you think would have happened if those guests would have been white, making those same statements about blacks?

There is a also a disparity in media coverage on crime, depending upon the race of the respective victims and perpetrators.

During the Tawana Brawley white-on-black false rape case, Al Sharpton protested constantly, all the time knowing the incident was a lie. Once the lie was exposed, the media quietly moved on to other stories and Sharpton suffered virtually no backlash.

On August 12, 2013 in Memphis, a white male nurse named David Santucci was confronted by three blacks while walking to his car. They killed him with a single shot through the heart with a 9mm pistol. The police department and the media (what little there was) called it a "robbery gone wrong", despite evidence to the contrary. First of all, he had not been robbed; none of his belongings were missing. Next, evidence showed he had been shot from about ten feet away, which is inconsistent with a robbery attempt. And finally, the shooter had numerous comments and pictures of alleged hate-crime victim Trayvon Martin on his Facebook page, indicating support for Martin. Witnesses said the shooter simply got out of his car, walked toward Santucci, fired the shot, then ran back to his car and drove off. Does that sound like a robbery attempt?

The George Zimmerman murder trial consumed the media for months. Ask yourself how many instances of black-on-white or black-on-black homicides were reported by the mainstream media during the Zimmerman trial? Did you hear about the murder of Christopher Cane? Or the stabbing of Natasha Martinez? How about the murder of 88-year-old World War II veteran Delbert Belton, who survived the Battle of Okinawa, only to be beaten to death by two black teenagers? Did you hear about the murder of ninety-nine-year-old Carol Jane Stergis? Or the murder of Melinda Schaefer? My guess is that you didn't hear of any of these. They were all as disturbing, if not more so, than the Trayvon Martin killing. The difference? All of the above killings had white victims and black assailants. The vast majority of interracial violent crimes are black-on-white. In fact, ninety percent of race-crime victims are white. Apparently, that doesn't sell papers.

The media never provides a breakdown by race when reporting on national homicide rates. Reports that portray the black community in a less-than-perfect light are scrubbed. The media reported that in 2010 the homicide-victim rate in the U.S. was 12.7 deaths per 100,000 population for males aged 10-24, and 2.1 deaths per 100,000 for females aged 10-24. What they didn't tell you is that the homicide rate was 2.9 deaths per 100,000 for white males aged 10-24 and 51.5 per 100,000 for black males aged 10-24. The homicide rate for blacks in that age group is more than seventeen times higher than for whites. Whites outnumber blacks by a five to one margin in population, yet blacks commit eight times more crimes against whites. That means that a black individual is forty times more likely to assault a white person than vice versa. Yet, whites are the ones accused of racism and hate crimes. Ignoring these facts will not accomplish anything.

Interracial rape is almost exclusively black-on-white. In 2007, an FBI study showed there were approximately 14,000 assaults on white women by black men. In contrast, there were less than ten assaults on black women by white men. You'll be hard-pressed to find those numbers in the mainstream media.

The Trayvon Martin Case

With as much publicity as the Trayvon Martin shooting generated, most people think they know the whole story. Unfortunately, most people don't. Here are the facts.

On the night of February 26, 2012, in the city of Sanford, Florida, a seventeen-year-old boy was shot by a twenty-eight-year-old man in an act of self-defense under Florida's "Stand Your Ground" laws. The boy, Trayvon Martin, was black. The shooter, George Zimmerman, was a mixed-race Hispanic.

Despite a preponderance of evidence supporting Zimmerman's claim of self-defense, and no evidence whatsoever indicating any racial motivation, the media turned this case into one of the most racially divisive cases in recent U.S. history.

In their efforts to create a hate crime, and sensationalize the story, the media resorted to a poorly planned game of smoke and mirrors. They started by portraying the shooting as an unjustified white-on-black hate crime, despite the fact that Zimmerman was Hispanic. The photos used in the media coverage consisted of a mug shot of Zimmerman, and a picture of Martin taken when he was only eleven years old. The intent was obvious. Next, *NBC* aired a recording of the 911 call, which it had edited to imply racial motivation. The narrative presented by the media was that of meek innocent little black child who was returning home from a local convenience store after buying some Skittles and an ice tea, when he was killed by a white racist. You've heard that version of the story.

Now comes the part the media didn't tell you.

At the time of the shooting, Trayvon Martin stood a muscular 5'11" tall. He played football and was a mixed-martial-arts fighter who boasted about how much he liked to make opponents bleed. He went by the twitter name "No Limit Nigga." Martin had been suspended from school three times for various offenses. One incident took place in October, 2011. A school police investigator said he observed Martin on a school surveillance camera in an unauthorized area "hiding and being suspicious." The recording showed Martin using a marker and writing "WTF", an acronym for "what the f*ck", on a locker door. The next day the officer searched Trayvon's book bag, looking for the marker. Instead, he found twelve pieces of women's jewelry, a watch, and what he described as a "burglary tool." The jewelry matched the items reported recently stolen from a residence just a few blocks from Krop Senior High School, which Martin attended. Trayvon was suspended for the graffiti, but never disciplined for the stolen jewelry. Why? Because the school had been involved in a manipulative scheme to improve the school's crime statistics by using school discipline rather than the Criminal Justice System, which would normally have been used in that situation. The jewelry was labeled as "Found Property", placed on a shelf in the property room, and never formally reported to the police. The Trayvon Martin case eventually led to the discovery of this scheme and the police chief was subsequently forced to resign.

Four months later, Martin was suspended for possession of a marijuana pipe and a baggy with marijuana residue.

According to his Twitter and Facebook conversations, Trayvon Martin was admittedly a user of marijuana and other lesser-known street drugs.

Remember the media's portrayal of Trayvon as an innocent boy coming home from the store with his Skittles and ice tea? Candy and ice tea seem very innocent, don't they? However, it wasn't just any old brand of ice tea . . . it was Arizona Watermelon Ice Tea. Do you know what you get when you mix Arizona Watermelon Ice Tea and Skittles with Robitussin DM or codeine cough syrup? You get a powerful PCP-like street drug called "lean" or "drank." If Robitussin DM is used, it is often referred to as "DXM." DXM is an abbreviation for the cough suppressant dextromethorphan hydrobromide, which is the active ingredient in Robitussin.

Trayvon Martin's social media posts suggest he was a frequent user of "lean" and was very adept at making it. Numerous social media posts by Martin included statements about using and manufacturing "lean", as well as searches for codeine cough syrup. George Zimmerman's testimony about Trayvon Martin's aggressive behavior would correlate with the reported side-effects of "lean" or "DXM", which can include breaks with reality, extreme paranoia, and fits of violence.

Martin's autopsy found marijuana in both his blood and urine. His liver showed the early stages of an unusual degrading known as "mild fatty metamorphosis," and his brain tissue appeared compromised—both conditions symptomatic of DXM use.

The facts paint a very different picture of this case. It's unfortunate that this young man had to die. It is equally unfortunate that the media ignored evidence and turned this into a hate crime, which likely spawned retaliatory assaults and homicides. This is just one example of irresponsible journalism. We need to start holding the media accountable.

Affirmative Action

Affirmative Action is fundamentally racist. It is based on the assumption that minorities are incapable of competing with whites. The goal was to increase minority representation in employment and education. Unfortunately, efforts to create racial balance and equalize results often produce side effects in which the harm outweighs any intended benefits. Regardless of intentions, affirmative action policies create new injustices with new victims. No person, regardless of skin color or ethnicity, should be turned away from educational opportunities, employment, scholarships, or career advancement based solely on the color of their skin.

Affirmative Action is really racial preference, and racial preferences often reinforce stereotypes of inequality and special treatment, and tarnish the legitimacy of one's achievements. This kind of discrimination was wrong fifty years ago, and it's still wrong today.

Colleges and universities often maintain separate admissions' standards and procedures for minority applicants, which is also discriminatory. Admissions to tax-payer-funded schools should go to those with adequate academic credentials, regardless of skin color or ethnicity. An "institution of higher learning" should not be a place where young men and women are taught that hard work and academic achievement can be trumped by skin color. A 2013 Washington Post/ABC News poll found that seventy-six percent of Americans from all races and political affiliations, opposed race-based college admissions.

Affirmative action is viewed by many as a form of reparation, which I personally do not believe in. It's unfair to discriminate against non-minorities who had nothing to do with past slavery or discriminatory practices, in order to benefit others who have never suffered from those offenses. How absurd is it to take jobs away from one group in order to compensate a second group for the purpose of correcting injustices caused by a third group who had mistreated a fourth group over 100 years ago? Think about that.

If you want fairness and equality, then we all need to play by the same rules. But, real diversity and equality takes work. Individuals are often reduced to skin color, ethnicity, or gender because those who champion diversity and equality usually want instant gratification and are unwilling to put forth the effort needed to achieve the optimum results.

Affirmative action regulations will continue to impact policy decisions and racial relations negatively. There are thousands of cases where people have worked hard and studied hard their entire lives, only to be passed over in favor of minorities with lesser qualifications. These are the real victims. These are the ones who have a legitimate complaint. The only thing an employer needs to know is one's ability, aptitude, work ethic, and character. And admittance to a university should be based on academic achievement, extra-curricular activities, ability, and character. Most of these victims don't complain. They simply utilize their work ethic and determination to find new opportunities.

If we are to realize Dr. King's vision, then we as a nation should not use skin color as a factor in determining a person's worthiness. Affirmative Action is a clear violation of Dr. King's ideology.

An Honest Opinion

Discussing the cultural problems that affect the black population is often unpleasant and uncomfortable. But, the issues can only be resolved if we are honest with ourselves about the causes. Hopefully, my opinion will be accepted in the spirit with which it is written.

One of the primary issues I see today is a tendency of inner-city blacks to accept the status quo and vilify those who don't. black individuality and exceptionalism are often frowned upon in those areas. Any African-American who wanders off the welfare plantation, to become articulate and academically successful, is often admonished and accused of being an "Uncle Tom."

Those who consider themselves victims have been brain-washed into believing their lot in life has been predetermined by some supreme racist power. But, racial discrimination has little to do with the major issues confronting African-Americans.

By comparison, the Asian population was also a race that was openly victimized and discriminated against throughout our early history. About 120,000 Japanese-Americans were sent to internment camps during World War II. Yet today, you find few Asians and Asian-Americans who are not successful. The Asian students do well in school. Many have had to learn English as a second language. The Asian unemployment rate is low. So, what do the Asians have that the African-Americans don't? One answer is simple . . . it's what they don't have. They don't have Jesse Jackson, Al Sharpton, The NAACP, or the Congressional Black Caucus telling them they are victims, and cannot rise above their current situation because the deck is stacked against them. They don't need affirmative action. They just go out and succeed because no one is there telling them they can't. They learn English because they understand that it is crucial in an English-Speaking country for self-improvement.

Many multiculturalist liberals want the country to be a "Celebration of Native Languages" and don't encourage mandatory English skills. The result is a huge number of minority high-school students performing scholastically at a sixth-grade level due to communication issues. You also end up with kids who are allowed to speak ebonics and wear their pants at half-mast, and lack proper mentorship on how to succeed in the real world. As a result, you have a recipe for long-term unemployment or underemployment once that student graduates.

Like it or not, society sets standards for most professional relationships. A person who has a sub-standard education and socially unacceptable behaviors or characteristics (improper dress, inability to speak effectively, poor hygiene, etc.) will suffer some form of bias in the workplace. Most jobs have generally accepted norms with regard to appearance and behavior. We are doing our children a disservice if we allow them to graduate without at least a fundamental understanding of these concepts.

Education is the single largest obstacle to the achievement of true equality. Yet, the Democrats are opposing school choice at the behest of the teachers' unions, which traps many children in sub-standard schools. The inferior quality of education in many African-American and Hispanic communities has lead to lower average achievement scores. If the black and Hispanic students in the U.S. performed at the same level as white and Asian students, the U.S. would lead all other nations in reading scores, and would trail only Japan in math and science. It is imperative that we give black children more educational opportunities.

Is The Tea Party Racist?

Liberals are always trying to convince me the Tea Party is racist. Yet, when I ask them what they base that assertion on, they never have an answer. So I felt compelled to include a short sub-chapter on the Tea Party, since they are the group most often accused of racism.

Let me start by stating I have no Tea Party Affiliation, although I do agree with most of their platform.

The mainstream media is all too eager to label the Tea Party as a bunch of old, white, male racists. From my observations, nothing could be further from the truth.

First of all, I have never seen a Tea Party member display even a hint of racism. In fact, the Tea Party appears to have one of the most diverse bases of any political party. Many of the Tea Party leaders and political candidates are hardly part of the "white establishment." Look at the names being thrown around as potential Presidential candidates: Ted Cruz, Marco Rubio, Ben Carson, Allen West, Herman Cain, Bobby Jindal, Tim Scott, Alan Keyes. No other party has a stable with that much diversity. The Tea Party has overwhelmingly supported minority candidates. There are many black Tea Party members, all of whom dispute the claims of racism within its membership, and if anyone should know, it would be them.

People have often attempted to "manufacture" the alleged racism. During a large Tea Party rally on Capitol Hill in 2010, to protest the Affordable Care Act, members of the Congressional Black Caucus, including Congressman John Lewis (D-GA) and Emmanuel Cleaver (D-MO) claimed they were subjected to numerous racial slurs and obscenities as they walked through the crowd of Tea Party members. Publisher and author Andrew Breitbart, convinced the Democrats had lied about the racist remarks, offered a $100,000.00 reward for any video or audio proof that supported the claims. Despite a sea of media cameramen and reporters, and tens of thousands of people with recording devices, not one frame of video or one recorded racist comment has been found to this day, which calls into question the integrity of the Congressional Black Caucus.

Americans of all races need to consider why the Tea Party exists in the first place. It has nothing to do with race, other than bringing races together for a common cause. The Tea Party principles of fiscal responsibility, limited government, a uniform rule of law, protection of personal rights and freedoms, school choice, educational accountability, elimination of excessive taxes, and civic responsibility, would be beneficial to all races. Their policies would certainly be far more beneficial to minorities than the current policies of Obama and the Democrats.

Tea Party members are simply conservatives trying to get America back on the right track. You can't fault them for that. The African-American community needs to fight this fight with the Tea Party, for the good of everyone.

Barack Hussein Obama

Prior to the election of Barack Obama as president in 2008, we were making significant progress toward living in a post-racial America. At that time, an *NBC News/Wall Street Journal* poll showed that seventy-nine percent of whites and sixty-three percent of blacks held a favorable opinion of race relations. The same poll, taken four and a half years into Obama's presidency, found those with a favorable opinion had dropped to fifty-two percent among whites and thirty-eight percent among blacks; a twenty-seven point and twenty-five point drop respectively. Several decades of progress had been erased in four-and-a-half years. And the gap has continued to widen. How could this have happened under the leadership of a man who billed himself as "The Great Unifier?" Race relations were supposed to get better. But, something happened on the way to the Kumbaya campfire. The answer is racism at the highest level.

A lot of white Americans, even many conservatives, voted for Obama, believing the election of the first black president would all but eliminate the country's remaining racial tensions. Unfortunately, people voted for Obama because it was historic, not because it was right. We all fell for Obama's message of unity, hope, and transparency, only to discover later that we had elected the most racially divisive president in history.

Most of the black community ignored Obama's associations with radical Anti-American groups, his lack of experience, and his commitment to push a Socialist agenda, believing that Obama's race outweighed any combination of negatives.

These days, there is an acceptable form of racism . . . voting for a political candidate based on the color of their skin. The fact that Barack Obama received ninety-six percent of the black vote in 2008, despite extremely poor qualifications, is, in essence, a form of racism. After four years of inept leadership and crippling policies, he still received ninety percent of the black vote in 2012, which is further proof that it's about color, not success. Voting for Obama because he was black was wrong, just as voting for an unqualified white candidate is wrong. You don't vote because it is historic, you vote for the person who is most qualified to lead the country.

If Barack Obama had been white, he would not have even won the primary, let alone the presidency. He would have been vetted properly and his lack of leadership and business experience would have cost him the nomination. Had he been white, the black community and the independents would not have ignored his associations with the likes of Bill Ayers and Bernadine Dohrn of the Weather Underground, communists Bea and Frank Lumpkin, convicted felon Tony Rezko, and communist Quentin Young. They would have been concerned about the impact of spending twenty years attending the Reverend Jeremiah Wright's church. One can only conclude that Obama remained a member of Wright's church because he believed in Wright's views.

Voters would have also been concerned that Obama's mentor for over nine years during his adolescence was racist Frank Marshall Davis, a key member of the United States Communist Party, who continued to be involved with Communist Party activities during his time with Obama. Anyone who thinks Frank Marshall Davis didn't try to fill young Barack's mind with propaganda is naïve.

The election of the first black president did not cure racial tensions. In reality, we lost ground. Having a black president has given the media and the Democratic Party the ability to claim racism any time Obama is criticized. Virtually any negative comment about Obama or his record is labeled "racism." Obama has allowed racist attitudes to flourish, as that is the glue that binds him to a segment of the African- American population. He tacitly encourages the mainstream media to accuse his political dissenters of racism. The media has complied, and has also turned a blind eye towards the actions of the Obama Administration with regard to racially divisive tactics.

Unfortunately, the Democratic Party and the race hustlers do not want an end to racial tension. It's part of the Saul Alynski divide-and-conquer mentality. That's why they consistently manufacture racial crises where there aren't any.

Another reason for the deterioration in race relations under Obama is the administration's constant undermining of situations with potential racial implications. During the Trayvon Martin murder trial, for example, most leaders would have sought to diffuse the racial unrest. Instead, the Obama Justice Department sent a unit with a history of anti-white racial advocacy to Sanford, Florida to help organize protests calling for George Zimmerman's prosecution, which included a rally headlined by Al Sharpton. Obama himself was later criticized for two very inappropriate statements, "If I had a son, he'd look like Trayvon" and "Trayvon Martin could have been me thirty-five years ago." He also indicated that if Trayvon had been white, the outcome would probably be different. Talk about throwing gas on the fire.

When members of the New Black Panther Party were filmed intimidating voters in front of a voting station in Philadelphia, Obama and Attorney General Eric Holder refused to prosecute the Black Panther members because they were black. Holder refers to blacks, including the Black Panthers, as "my people." As the U.S. Attorney General, shouldn't everyone in America be "his people?"

In February 2014, Obama unveiled an initiative known as "My Brother's Keeper," a program aimed at "empowering" boys and young men of color. Once again, we have a program that is reactive rather than pro-active, and overtly discriminatory. This program does nothing for any disadvantaged white youth, nor does it address disadvantaged minority girls and young women. It also fails to address the primary issue, which is a failing inner-city public education system. Obama was instrumental in killing a popular and effective school voucher program in Washington D.C., which ruined the opportunity for many poor black families to get out of the D.C. public school system, one of the worst in the country. His allegiance to the teachers unions apparently overrides his concern for poor black families. It's ironic that President Obama would initiate a program like "My Brother's Keeper" while his own half-brother, George Hussein Obama, lives in a corrugated tin shack in the slums of Nairobi, battling drug and alcohol addictions. There has been no "hope" and no "change" for George Obama. George actually had to ask filmmaker Dinesh D'Souza for $1,000.00 to cover medical expenses for his sick child, which D'Souza gladly gave him. That amounted to $1,000.00 more than he received from his brother, Barack.

Obama's walk doesn't match the talk. His fixation on "social justice" has made racial tensions worse. And he has been allowed to act with virtual impunity as the media and his fellow Democrats are in lockstep with his every move. They accept everything he says without question. Obama claimed his very conception was the result of the love affair between his mother and father during the civil rights march on Selma, Alabama, a story which the media and Democrats readily accepted. The only problem is that Obama was born in 1961, his parents divorced in 1964, and the march on Selma happened in 1965. Apparently, honesty and accuracy are not high on his or the media's list of values.

Recently, however, the tide has begun to turn. More and more Democrats and members of the African-American community are beginning to realize Obama's policies and ideology have worsened their social and economic ills. After six years of Obama, George W. Bush can no longer be the scapegoat.

African-Americans Under Obama

Surveys taken during the summer of 2014 showed that President Obama's approval rating was at all-time lows, averaging in the low forty-percent range among all registered voters. He was also cited in a poll as the worst president in modern history. Yet, at the same time, his approval rating among black voters was in the mid eighty-percent range. This is a shocking statistic considering the negative socio-economic impact Obama's policies have had on the average African-American citizen.

I, like most people, wanted Barack Obama to be successful as president. I judge a president's success by how the average American's quality of life is impacted, so any president's success, regardless of color or political affiliation, is a good thing.

Unfortunately, President Obama's policies have hurt virtually every sector of the populace, with blacks being hurt the most.

According to the latest available Census Bureau numbers, 14.3 percent of Americans were below the poverty line when Obama took office, compared to 15.0 percent in 2012. Black Americans went from 25.8 to 27.2 percent.

That same report also indicates that inflation-adjusted median household income among blacks dropped from $34,880.00 to $33,321.00 during that same period, and blacks were already well below the national average. In the last few years, the black middle-class has experienced one of the largest losses of wealth ever.

Home ownership among African-Americans dropped from 46.1 to 43.3 percent during Obama's first four years.

The latest Department of Agriculture statistics show that during Obama's first term, the number of food stamp recipients in America increased from 32,889,999 to over forty-six million, a twenty-nine percent increase. The number of blacks on food stamps increased by thirty-three percent, from 7,393,000, when Obama took office in 2009, to 10,955,000 in 2012.

According to the Bureau of Labor Statistics, the jobs numbers for blacks are equally dismal. When Obama took office, the unemployment rate for blacks was 12.7 percent. The most recent BLS report shows a black unemployment rate of 11.5 percent, and the media is quick to point out the 1.2 percentage point drop. What they don't tell you is that between January, 2009 and May, 2014, the labor participation rate among blacks dropped from 63.2 to 60.8 percent, with 1.8 million blacks leaving the workforce since Obama took office. If those people were added back into the workforce, the current unemployment rate among blacks would be over twenty-one percent. Black unemployment is more than double white unemployment.

The latest BLS report also shows that the unemployment rate for black women is higher now than when Obama took office—up from 9.2 percent to the current ten percent. One-hundred-twenty-nine thousand more African-American women are unemployed.

Now, add to that the impact of Obama's proposed immigration and amnesty plans. A flood of low-skilled immigrants will make it even more difficult for all Americans to compete for low-skilled jobs. Studies have shown that African-Americans are disproportionately harmed by immigration and amnesty. A report published by the National Bureau of Economic Research determined that the immigrant influx between 1980-2000 increased the number of workers in the U.S. by nearly ten percent, and accounted for about forty percent of the 17.9 percentage point decline in black employment rates.

On the education front, the Obama administration has been against charter schools and tuition voucher programs, which have been a lifeline for thousands of poor black children. In Louisiana, for example, the Justice Department recently filed a lawsuit against the state's tuition voucher program, arguing that it might compromise desegregation efforts, despite the fact that ninety percent of the children receiving vouchers are black.

In reference to President Obama, Harry Alford, president of the National Black Chamber of Commerce, recently stated, "I don't know how much he has done or how much his policies are responsible for the current state of blacks in America. What I do know is that we are worse off than we were when he came into office."

Does the African-American community fully understand the negative impact this administration has had on their lives, or are they giving him a pass because he is the first black president? Americans of all races and parties would never have allowed a white president, regardless of political affiliation, to get away with the kind of divisiveness and ineptness that this president has shown. However, until we are brave enough to bring an honest discussion to the table, and address the real issues which are impacting the African-American community, it is doubtful the situation will improve.

In Their Own Words

"We have to exterminate white people off the face of the planet." Black Professor Kamau Kambow

"I say in the words of Malcom X, if you find any good white people, kill them now before they turn bad." Quanell X black

Author & Radio personality during an interview on the O'Reilly Factor

"... the white Liberals who have been posing as our friends have failed us." Malcom X

"Anytime you throw your political weight behind a political party that controls two-thirds of the government and that party can't keep the promises it made to you during election time, and you are dumb enough to walk around and identify yourself with that party, you are not only a chump, but you are a traitor to your race." Malcom X

"Obama is electable because he is light-skinned with no Negro dialect." Democratic Senator Harry Reid

"I'll have those niggers voting Democrat for the next 200 years." President Lyndon Johnson

"Rather I should die a thousand times, and see Old Glory trampled in the dirt never to rise again, than to see this beloved land of ours become degraded by race mongrels, a throwback to the blackest specimen from the wilds." Robert Byrd, Democrat Senator (1959 - 2010)

"... it is race prejudice, I guess. But I am strongly of the opinion Negroes ought to be in Africa, Yellow men in Asia and White men in Europe and America." Democrat President Lyndon Johnson

"Civil Rights laws were not passed to protect the rights of white men and do not apply to them." Mary Frances Berry Democratic Chair, U.S. Commission on Civil Rights

"These Negroes, they're getting pretty uppity these days and that's a problem for us since they've got something now they never had before, the political pull to back up their uppity-ness. Now we've got to do something about this, we've got to give them a little something, just enough to quiet them down, not enough to make a difference." Democrat President Lyndon Johnson

"Mahatma Gandhi 'ran a gas station down in St. Louis." Senator Hillary Clinton

"Blacks and Hispanics are 'too busy eating watermelons and tacos' to learn how to read and write." Mike Wallace, *CBS News*

"I think one man is just as good as another so long as he's not a nigger or a Chinaman. Uncle Will says that the Lord made a white man from dust, a nigger from mud, then he threw up what was left and it came down a Chinaman." Democrat President Harry Truman in a letter to his wife, Bess.

Conclusion

Socio-economic problems within various ethnic demographics are often challenging and difficult to talk about. Allowing the media and political groups to incorrectly attribute those problems to racism and racial discrimination creates an even larger issue. True racists account for only a small portion of Americans, despite what the race mongers and the media tell us. However, the fear of being accused of racism is a powerful tool, and the ability to utilize this tool has given the Left a hold over a significant portion of the electorate. Although both whites and blacks agree that anti-black racism has decreased over the last sixty years, there is still a large demographic where racism continues to be a conditioned response. There doesn't seem to be a unilateral racism. The self-identification of victimhood and perceived racism appears to occur more often in the lower socio-economic segments of the black community, where civil rights leaders, politicians, and the liberal elite have all benefited from giving African-Americans the impression they are being continuously victimized. These groups focus exclusively on defending the "rights" of the black offenders rather than condemning the violence they commit.

The mainstream media is filled with editorials and opinion pieces that try to convince the poor minorities they are destined to remain in poverty, with few options for success, and therefore, by osmosis, must remain relegated to a dependency on the welfare system.

This approach does nothing to eliminate the remaining remnants of racism. Ending racism needs to come from the heart, not the pocketbook. We need to be honest with ourselves rather than spend money on short-term fixes. The African-American community shouldn't have survived centuries of slavery and racism only to become victims of a welfare state.

People of all races can, and will, succeed if allowed to utilize their talents and ideas without government interference or negative re-enforcement from race mongers. Programs like "My Brother's Keeper" and Affirmative Action need to go away. Any program that divides mankind based on ethnicity, is destined to erode any progress we have made and undermine the American dream. We need to remember there was never a promise of equal outcomes by Martin Luther King, only the promise of equal opportunities.

We're not living the dream Dr. King envisioned. If we want to realize that dream, we have to be honest with ourselves, and create an open dialog. Have you ever heard any of this information before? You may have heard some, but not a lot. Because the media doesn't report it, the teachers don't teach it, and the Left doesn't repeat it.

We are at a point in time where ideology and political correctness have stifled open dialog and discussion of opposing views. Any reasonable discussion should not be forced to yield to political correctness. The truth will always remain the truth, and no amount of sugar-coating can change it.

We need to be more assertive in calling out the real racists. No group or individual espousing racism, in any form, should be immune to criticism. As long as people of all races confidently stand together and support our core values and beliefs, we will be one giant step closer to unifying this great country. Let us all be judged on the content of our character.

CHAPTER FOUR

Gun Control

Gun control is one of those issues where you either "get it" or you don't. Those of us who grew up around guns understand the need and the desire to own guns. We were taught gun safety and usage. We know guns are simply a tool, and like any tool, can be dangerous if not used properly. Many gun-control proponents know nothing about guns. Although their intentions are good, they have not been given enough factual information to make an informed assessment. Most have never fired a gun, whether hunting, target practicing, or using one in self-defense. Many are afraid of guns and have decided they have no use for them. Their rationale for limiting or banning guns is to reduce accidental shootings and keep guns out of the hands of criminals—which is a very naïve and dangerous mindset. Criminals will always have access to guns. Restricting guns will only create a larger pool of defenseless victims. Literally millions of assaults, rapes, murders, and robberies have been thwarted by average citizens who were fortunate enough to have guns with which to defend themselves.

The mainstream media and a large portion of academia are filled with anti-gun idealists, putting pro-gun Americans at an informational disadvantage. The media is notorious for cherry-picking data to support its anti-gun narrative. However, when all of the data is provided, it paints a very different picture.

The primary question in the gun control debate is, "Would gun-control laws reduce gun crimes or lower murder rates?"

Based on historical data, gun control is more likely to escalate violent crime, including murder. States and counties with the strictest gun laws tend to have higher rates of overall crime, including gun crime. Chicago, which has extremely strict gun regulations, has the highest number of gun homicides in the country. Historically, murder rates have increased in every area that has banned all guns, or banned handguns. The number of gun-related homicides has dropped in a few instances, but the overall murder rate has risen.

Gun control only affects law-abiding citizens. Criminals usually get their guns illegally, through theft, black-market purchase, or purchase through a third party. During the prohibition, people who wanted alcohol were able to get it, easily. The same is true for guns. Let's face it, if someone wants to kill you, or use a weapon in the commission of a crime, they will find an alternative. Of all the largest mass-killings in United States history, most did not involve a gun. I will discuss this in greater depth later in the chapter.

Mass killings are rare, so they get more media coverage, especially if a gun was used. But overall, there has not been an increase in instances or victims. You will always have mentally ill people, many with no outward signs of illness. Until we can adequately address the problem of mental illness, there will likely be more mass killings in the future, regardless of our attempts to prevent them. Some measures that are taken actually seem to be counter- productive. Do you think it is a coincidence that almost all of the mass-shootings have taken place in "gun-free" zones? Mass killers may be mentally unstable, but they know enough to carry out their atrocities in areas that are generally devoid of armed citizens. The equation changes when they know there is an increased likelihood of being confronted by an armed citizen.

Guns are an equalizer. The police are not always going to be right around the corner. If a criminal broke into your mother's or your grandmother's home with the intent of raping and murdering her, and every second counted, would you want her to have a gun to defend herself with, or a phone to call 911? What if there were multiple assailants? Would you want her to only have six bullets in her gun? Do you know for a fact that, during an assault, you could stop even one assailant with six bullets, allowing for missed shots due to the chaos of the situation?

Tactical-style weapons and high-capacity magazines are a favorite target of the anti-gun lobby. Yet those weapons are seldom used in homicides. Why ban high-capacity magazines? The criminals will still be able to get high-capacity clips if they want them. The result of banning these types of magazines is a victim who runs out of bullets before the assailant. See what happens when you scream out "hold on guys, I have to reload."

Has anyone ever presented you with undeniable proof that tighter gun control laws reduce murder and violent crime? Anti-gun activists' arguments use opinions rather than facts. In most cases, they don't have any idea what the facts are. Allow me to provide you with a few.

The Statistics

As stated earlier, the mainstream media cherry-picks the information it chooses to report with regard to gun crimes. The information they neglect to report tells an entirely different story.

For example, using the latest available statistics, the media reports that more than 32,000 Americans are killed by gun violence every year. What most fail to report is that sixty-one percent of those deaths were suicides, and twenty-eight percent were gang-related. An additional three percent were accidental shootings, two percent were in self-defense, and six percent were classified as "other."

Actual gun "homicides" totaled just over 11,000, of which approximately 8800 were gang-related. The rate of firearm homicide deaths was 3.6 per 100,000 people, which puts the United States in the middle of all countries worldwide. Honduras was the highest at 68.4 per 100,000 people.

If the gang-related gun homicides were excluded from the U.S. total, we would actually rank below Switzerland, which is well below one per 100,000.

In 1960, there were a total of approximately 77.5 million privately-owned guns in the United States, with a total population of about 179 million people. Based on those figures, there was one gun for every 2.31 people. The murder rate in 1960 was 5.1 per 100,000 people.

In 2012, the number of privately-owned guns had increased to an estimated 333 million, based on estimates from the Bureau of Alcohol Tobacco and Firearms. The U.S. population had increased to approximately 316 million people. This puts the current gun ownership ratio at just over one per person, more than double the 1960 ratio. Yet, the murder rate in 2012 was only 4.7 per 100,000 people, including gang-related killings, which weren't as prevalent in 1960.

The murder rate has actually dropped substantially despite a huge increase in firearms, and despite a significant increase in gang-related gun deaths.

When the 1994 Federal Assault Weapons Ban expired in 2004, the murder rate was 5.5 per 100,000. If assault weapons play such a key role in the murder rate, why has the murder rate declined since the expiration of the ban?

Overall, the statistics continue to show that cities and states with the strictest gun control laws have the most gun violence. In states that have right-to-carry laws, the murder rate is twenty-eight percent lower than in states that don't. Violent crime is twenty-four percent lower.

In 1977, a handgun ban went into effect in Washington, D.C. The ban also included a requirement that other firearms be kept unloaded and disassembled. Since the ban took effect, there has only been one year that the murder rate fell below pre-ban levels. In fact, D.C. ranked among the top four major cities in the U.S. for the highest annual murder rate nineteen times, earning the nickname "Murder Capital."

And, despite having some of the toughest gun laws in the country, Washington D.C. had a rate of 1508 violent crimes per 100,000 people.

Massachusetts passed strict gun laws in 1998, a year in which there were sixty-five gun homicides statewide. From 1998 to 2011, armed robbery rose 20.7 percent, and aggravated assaults rose 26.7 percent. In 2011, there were 122 gun homicides in Massachusetts. While the overall murder rate for the country was falling, Massachusetts' homicide rates were climbing. Rather than admit their gun-control measures weren't working, the increase was blamed on the neighboring states' failure to enact similar restrictions. This excuse can be easily debunked. In 1998, the murder rate in Massachusetts equaled only about seventy percent of the murder rate of its neighbors (New York, Rhode Island, Vermont, New Hampshire, Maine, and Connecticut). It has since risen to one-hundred-twenty-five percent of that rate.

Gun homicide rates for the U.S. were 3.6 per 100,000 people, based on the most recent available statistics. The top ten major cities for gun homicides per capita are as follows:

New Orleans	-	62.1 per 100,000 people
Detroit	-	35.9 per 100,000 people
Baltimore	-	29.7 per 100,000 people

Newark	-	25.4 per 100,000 people
Washington DC	-	19.0 per 100,000 people
Atlanta	-	17.2 per 100,000 people
Cleveland	-	17.4 per 100,000 people
Buffalo	-	16.5 per 100,000 people
Houston	-	12.9 per 100,000 people
Chicago	-	11.6 per 100,000 people

These ten cities alone accounted for approximately twelve percent of the total U.S. gun homicides. They all share one thing in common. They are all Democrat-controlled cities with strict gun laws.

By comparison, Utah, which the Brady Campaign determined to have the least gun control, had a gun homicide rate of less than one percent.

In Illinois, the concealed-carry ban was lifted, effective January 2014. Not surprisingly, the murder rate in Chicago plummeted. Through August 2014, the murder rate was down nine percent from the same period in 2013, and twenty-seven percent from 2012.

Larger urban areas usually have lower rates of gun ownership than rural areas, but significantly higher murder rates. Chicago, a city with a low gun-ownership rate, had 506 murders in 2012 and 440 in 2013. These numbers may actually be higher, based on a story published in *Chicago Magazine* in April 2014, which was one of the best pieces of investigative journalism I have seen in recent years.

The United States has the highest level of gun ownership in the world. To think that confiscating or reducing the number of legal guns will decrease gun violence is naïve. As I stated earlier, it's easy for criminals to get illegal guns. In the first six months of

2014, in Chicago alone, police seized more than 3,300 illegal firearms. That is only a fraction of what is in Chicago. Imagine the number nationally.

When criminals don't feel threatened by armed citizens, it also changes the dynamics of their crimes. In the U.K., nearly half of all burglaries are committed while the victim is home, compared to only thirteen percent in the United States. An unarmed victim being home significantly increases the odds of something going terribly wrong.

More attention needs to be paid to existing laws and punishments. Repeat offenders make up the bulk of murderers in the United States. In his book *More Guns, Less Crime*, John Lott reported that in 1988, in the seventy-five largest counties in the U.S., more than eighty-nine percent of adult murderers had a prior criminal record. Just as disturbing, between February 2004 and February 2010, there were a total of 1,225 background checks done for firearms, and three for explosives, for people who were on terrorist watch lists. Despite these checks, all of the explosive transactions, and ninety-one percent of the firearms transactions, were allowed.

Finally, as I mentioned before, a vast majority of the gun homicides in the U.S. are gang-related. The national Youth Gang Survey Analysis found that total gang members in the U.S. are forty-nine percent Hispanic, thirty-five percent black, and ten percent white.

The media is quick to point out gun homicides when the offender is white. They will spend days, sometimes weeks, on those stories. But when the offender is not white, it receives generally little media attention.

In their effort to be politically correct, the media never points out crime statistics from a "cultural" viewpoint. In New York, ninety-eight percent of all gun crime is committed by blacks and Hispanics. World-wide homicide rate rankings are dominated by Latin-American countries. Yet, some people want us to open our borders to illegals from Latin American countries, including thousands of gang members, without a hint of due diligence.

Defensive Gun Use

The media always points out the harm firearms inflict, but they seldom mention the benefits. There have been literally millions of instances of defensive gun use, which prevented untold numbers of violent crime, including murder, rape, and armed robbery. These are crimes that would not have been prevented if the potential victims had not been armed. It's difficult to arrive at an estimate of defensive gun use incidents in the United States, but published reports give estimates of between 108,000 and 3.6 million annually.

Of the reports surveyed for this book, the most legitimate report on defensive gun use appears to be a report written by Gary Kleck, a Florida State University criminologist, based on his study done in the 1990s. This is the most comprehensive survey to-date. After reviewing eleven prior surveys, all of which were flawed to some degree, Kleck conducted his own survey, designed specifically to arrive at a more accurate representation. Kleck's study, the National Self-Defense Survey, interviewed 4977 random people in the forty-eight contiguous states. The final results showed that 1.125 percent of the adults surveyed had used guns defensively an average of 1.472 times each. Based on the population of the United States at that time, this equated to approximately 2.16 million defensive gun uses per year.

Only twenty-four percent of the respondents actually fired their guns, and only eight- percent thought the assailant had been wounded. The respondent was injured in eleven of the cases, and each only used his gun *after* being attacked.

Another report done that same year, the National Crime Victimization Survey (NCVS), estimated only 108,000 defensive gun uses annually. However, this report has several drawbacks.

First, it is conducted as part of a larger overall survey, and not designed to pinpoint defensive gun uses. Secondly, it is conducted by the Census Bureau, which means the results are based on households, rather than individuals. Finally, many people are reluctant to provide firearm data to a government agency, for a variety of reasons. Some people will not report defensive gun use because they are in an area where guns, including theirs, are prohibited. Others simply feel it is none of the government's business.

The Department of Justice sponsored a survey the following year, using a smaller sample size than Kleck, and arrived at an estimate of 1.5 million defensive gun uses annually. That means for every gun homicide that is not gang-related, there are approximately 680 defensive gun uses, based on their figures. Even using the NCVS figures, which are arguably low, you still have at least forty-nine defensive gun uses for every non-gang-related gun homicide.

Also, there are a number of other residual benefits we can't see. Often, criminals will flee, once they know a potential victim is armed, before any crime occurs. And, keep in mind, a victim who shoots an assailant, or holds them until the police arrive, may have prevented many more attacks. These would not, of course, be counted statistically.

The National Institute of Justice surveyed prison inmates on the subject of defensive gun use by potential victims. The survey found that at least thirty-four percent had been deterred by an armed victim. Another seventy percent knew a fellow criminal who had been deterred because a gun had been present.

In a study done by the National Crime Survey, robberies succeed eighty-eight percent of the time, and victims are injured twenty-five percent of the time, when a victim does not defend himself and/or his property. However, when the victim defends himself with a gun, the robbery success rate drops to thirty percent and the victim injury rate drops to seventeen-percent.

Speaking From Experience

Those who advocate for gun control often assume anyone who is against gun control has never been a victim, or has never lost someone to gun violence. There are cases, I'm sure, where that is true. I don't know the statistics, but I can speak from experience: it certainly isn't always true.

On the evening of May 8, 1981 I was in a tavern in Salem, Oregon called the Oregon Museum. It was a Thursday night and I was with some guys from my softball team, having a beer and socializing after an earlier practice game. There were about a hundred people in the bar, and I knew about a third of them. After the band began playing, several of us decided to go home and get cleaned up, then return to the club, where we would normally hang out until about midnight.

I drove straight to my house, about five miles from the Museum, and the drive took about twenty minutes. As I was changing clothes, my home phone rang. When I answered, the voice on the other end said, "Thank God you're okay." It was a friend calling to tell me a man had just shot a bunch of people at the Museum. I headed back to the club, but the police had it cordoned off. I found out later that three of my friends had been killed, and seven of my friends had been wounded. In all, four people were killed and twenty injured. The shooter, Lawrence "Larry" Moore, had emptied two clips from a 9mm pistol into the crowd. Even though I lost three friends (Johnny Cooper, Eric Hamblin, and Lori Cunningham), I never once felt the gun or its availability was the problem. Larry went there to kill people that night. If a gun hadn't been available, he would have found another way—one that may have even been more horrific.

I often wonder what the outcome would have been if one of the patrons who stayed would have been armed. I am positive the victim toll would have been less. That's my opinion.

You Don't Need a Gun To Kill

The media is fixated on an anti-gun agenda, and is determined to spin all of their reporting on gun violence to promote that agenda. They tell us mass shootings are skyrocketing and strict gun-control regulations need to be enacted. They hammer us with Newtown, Columbine, Virginia Tech, and the Aurora movie-theatre shootings. We know who Adam Lanza, Dylan Klebold, Eric Harms, James Holmes, and Jared Loughner are. But the media doesn't look any further, and we don't seem to care.

All the reporting, and all the so-called solutions, are reactive rather than proactive. We need to address the source of the problems. Someone who wants to kill will always be able to kill. The method used is irrelevant. Much of the crime in America, including mass shootings, is a product of broken homes, gang violence, inner-city deterioration, absentee parents, and mental illness. Unless these issues are dealt with proactively, things will never improve. It is not the gun we need to deal with.

California, the poster child for anti-gun legislation, couldn't stop Elliot Rodger. Despite having arguably the toughest gun laws in America, and earning an "A" rating from the Brady Campaign and the Law Center to Prevent Gun Violence, Elliot Rodger killed seven people, including himself, and injured thirteen others on the campus of U.C. Santa Barbara. As much as the media wanted to blame the gun, the problem was the person. Three of the victims were actually stabbed to death. Outwardly, Elliot Rodger appeared to have no issues, though he had been receiving psychiatric treatment for years. At the request of his mother, the police had questioned Rodger shortly before the killings. They reported that Rodger appeared to be "quiet and timid, polite and courteous." As such, the home was never searched. His three semi-automatic pistols and 137-page manifesto were never found. The rest is history.

There were seven mass shootings in 2012, including Sandy Hook and the Aurora theatre killings. Mental illness played a role in each. Connecticut has one of the strictest gun laws in the nation, which did nothing to stop Adam Lanza. Almost everything Adam Lanza did that day was illegal, i.e. theft, murder, firearm on school grounds, trespassing, assault. Why would he care about breaking the law? He was going out to kill people.

Steven Kazmierczak killed five students and wounded twenty-one others on the Northern Illinois University campus on Valentine's Day in 2008. He used a shotgun and three handguns. He had an extensive history of mental illness, but had been out of the system for five years, so he could legally buy guns. This is where the system is failing.

Basically, background checks will only reveal the criminals. Mentally ill people with no criminal history, and no available medical history, would not be stopped.

Of the most prolific mass-murders in U.S. history, the majority did not use a gun. The tragedy of 9/11 killed 2996 people and injured more than 6000 without a single shot being fired. The terrorists used box cutters and planes.

On April 19, 1995, Timothy McVeigh used fertilizer and diesel fuel to kill 168 and injure 680 others.

On March 25, 1990, arson killed 87 people at Happy Land, a social club in The Bronx, N.Y.

The worst school massacre in U.S. history was committed using explosives. The massacre took place in 1927 in Bath, Michigan. Thirty-eight children, two teachers, and four others were killed. Fifty-eight people were injured.

Gary Ridgway, the Green River killer, confessed to seventy-one murders. None of the victims were killed with a gun.

John Wayne Gacy committed at least thirty-three murders without a gun.

The top five serial killers in the world, Louis Garavito, Pedro Lopez, Daniel Camago, Pedro Rodriques Filho, and Abul Djabar, are suspected of killing a combined total of more than 1250 people, none of which were killed with a gun.

Finally, according to Grant Duwe, author of *Mass Murder in the United States: A History*, the overall number of mass murders in the United States dropped from forty-three cases in the 1990s to twenty-six over the following ten years. The increased number of mass shootings in 2012 appears to have been an anomaly. You will never read about the mass killings that were prevented by armed citizens.

Around The World

Statistics show that stricter gun control laws have led to increased crime in the U.S., but how about worldwide?

The United Kingdom enacted the Firearms Act of 1998, following the mass killing of seventeen people at an elementary school in Dublane, Scotland two years earlier. This act resulted in a nearly complete ban on handguns. During the first decade after the law was implemented, gun violence spiked dramatically, especially among gangs. The homicide rate reversed only after the police force was expanded substantially. Many British police now carry guns.

Honduras had few gun laws prior to 1985, at which point it changed from a military dictatorship to a democracy, and firearms became increasingly regulated. A national gun registry was created and assault weapons were banned. Individuals were limited to five guns. Honduras now leads the world in gun homicides at 68.4 per 100,000 people, compared to 3.6 per 100,000 in the United States.

Russia has extremely strict gun-control laws, yet the murder rate in Russia per capita is much higher than that of the United States.

Mexico has one of the strictest gun laws in the world, yet the gun homicide rate is almost three times higher than in the U.S.

Brazil, which also has extremely strict gun laws, has a gun-homicide rate of 18.1 per 100,000 people, five times higher than that of the United States.

Switzerland, New Zealand, Finland and Israel, all have high gun-ownership levels and comparatively less restrictive gun laws, but all have gun-homicide rates under one per 100,000 people.

The U.S. media forgets to mention that other countries, with strict gun laws, have mass killings and injuries, just like we have had. In China, where there are very strict gun laws, and fewer than one gun for every twenty people, mass killings and injuries are just as prolific. Here are some examples:

> On March 23, 2010, a knife-wielding man killed eight and wounded several others at an elementary school in China's Fujian Province.

> On April 28, 2010 at the Hong Fu Primary School in Leizhou, Guangdong, thirty-three-year-old Chen Kangbing wounded sixteen students and a teacher with a knife.

> On April 29, 2010 at Zhongxin Kindergarten in Taixing, Jiangsu, a forty-seven-year-old man stabbed 28 students, two teachers and a security guard.

> On April 30, 2010, a man named Wang Younlai injured several preschool children with a hammer in Shandong province.

> On May 12, 2010, a forty-eight-year-old man used a meat cleaver to kill seven children and two adults, and injured eleven others in Hanzhong, Shaanxi.

> On August 4, 2010 a twenty-six-year-old man killed three children and a teacher, and injured about twenty others at a kindergarten.

In August 2011, eight children were injured with a box-cutter by a woman at a childcare center in Shanghia where she worked.

In September 2011, a man in Henan Province used an axe to kill a young girl and three adults. Two others were injured.

In December 2012, a thirty-six-year-old man in Henan Province used a knife to injure twenty-three children and an elderly woman at the Chempeng Village Primary School.

In August 2012, a teenager in northeast China used a knife to kill eight people and wound five others.

On June 7, 2013, a man with a can of gas started a fire on a crowded bus in Xiamen, Fugian Province, killing forty-seven and injuring thirty-four.

Most recently, in March of 2014, ten men in China, armed with knives, killed twenty-nine people and injured 130 in a train station in Kunming.

All of these mass killings and injuries had one thing in common: none of the assailants used a gun.

In Their Own Words

"All vets are mentally ill in some sort of way and government should prevent them from owning firearms." Democrat Senator Dianne Feinstein, to the Senate Judiciary Committee

"This year will go down in history. For the first time, a civilized nation has full gun registration. Our streets will be safer, our police more efficient, and the world will follow our lead into the future!" Adolph Hitler

"The biggest hypocrites on gun control are those who live in upscale developments with armed security guards —and who want to keep other people from having guns to defend themselves. But, what about lower-income people, living in high-crime, inner-city neighborhoods? Should such people be kept unarmed and helpless, so the limousine liberals can make a statement by adding to the thousands of gun laws already on the books?" Thomas Sowell

"Gun control? It's the best thing you can do for crooks and gangsters. I want you to have nothing. I'm a bad guy; I'm always gonna have a gun. Safety locks? You will pull the trigger with a lock on, and I'll pull the trigger [without one]. We'll see who wins." Sammy "The Bull" Gravano, whose testimony convicted John Gotti.

"Have you ever heard of a mass shooting in a police station, at a pistol range, or at a gun show? Suicidal mass murderers may be insane, but they are not necessarily stupid. They always select a soft target for their final acts of violence. This principle also applies to many other types of crime" Michael S. Brown, *The Tragedy of Gun Free Zones*

"Let me make a point here, in case this isn't becoming extremely clear. My state has gun-control laws. It did not keep Hennard from coming in and killing everybody! What it did do, was keep me from protecting my family! That's the only thing that cotton pickin' law did! OK! Understand that! That's . . . that's so important!" Suzanna Gratia Hupp; Killeen, Texas; Luby's massacre survivor

"Strict gun laws are about as effective as strict drug laws . . . It pains me to say this, but the NRA seems to be right: The cities and states that have the toughest gun laws have the most murder and mayhem." Mike Royko, *Chicago Tribune*

"Gun control has not worked in D.C. The only people who have guns are criminals. We have the strictest gun laws in the nation and one of the highest murder rates. It's quicker to pull your Smith & Wesson than to dial 911 if you're being robbed." Lt. Lowell Duckett, *The Washington Post*, March 22, 1996

"As a card-carrying member of the liberal media, producing this piece was an eye opening experience. I have to admit that I saw guns as inherently evil, violence begets violence, and so on. I have learned, however, that in trained hands, just the presence of a gun can be a real "man stopper." I am sorry that women have had to resort to this, but wishing it wasn't so won't make it any safer out there." Jill Fieldstein, *CBS* producer, *Street Stories: Women and Guns*

"Democracy is two wolves and a lamb voting on what to have for lunch. Liberty is a well-armed lamb contesting the outcome of the vote." Benjamin Franklin

"Gun control: The theory that a woman found dead in an alley, raped and strangled with her panty hose, is somehow morally superior to a woman explaining to police how her attacker got that fatal bullet wound." L. Neil Smith

"In the debate over guns, both sides are angry. The pro-gunners are angry at the ignorance, lies, and distortions of the anti-gunners, and the anti-gunners for presenting facts." Dave Champion

"They have gun control in Cuba. They have universal health care in Cuba. So why do they want to come here?" Paul Harvey, 1994

"We would just go out and line up a bunch of cans and shoot with rifles, handguns and at times, submachine guns . . . When I was a kid it was a controlled atmosphere, we weren't shooting at humans . . . we were shooting at cans and bottles mostly. I will most certainly take my kids out for target practice." Johnny Depp

"In a comprehensive study of all public multiple shooting incidents in America between 1977 and 1999, economists John Lott and Bill Landes found that the only public policy that reduced both the incidence and casualties of such shootings were concealed-carry laws. Not only are there 60 percent fewer gun massacres after states adopt concealed-carry laws, but the death and injury rate of such rampages are reduced by 80 percent." Ann Coulter

Conclusion

Gun control is not about controlling guns—it's about controlling people. If people are unable to defend themselves, they will feel the need to seek that protection from the government. But, what happens if that government goes against the will of the people?

The purpose of the 2nd Amendment was to give the citizenry the ability to overthrow an oppressive government, should one arise, and an individual's right to self-defense. The Supreme Court interpreted the 2nd Amendment to mean that firearms which are in common use cannot be banned, and that the amendment protects the individual's right to keep and bear arms for "traditionally lawful purposes." Once we start losing gun rights, the gun-control advocates won't stop. Incremental restrictions will continue until all semblance of gun-rights have disappeared. The U.K. is considering banning steak knives!

Gun-control advocates rely on the apathy of many independents and moderates, and the ignorance of those on the Left who know absolutely nothing about guns, other than what they've read. That includes the people who are making our laws. It's amazing that people who know so little about guns can declare themselves authorities on the subject, and support their beliefs without solid evidence. People who know nothing about guns should not be responsible for creating gun legislation.

Anti-gun lobbyists argue that guns are too accessible, despite the fact there are background checks, waiting periods, registration, fingerprinting, etc. Yet, fifty years ago, you could buy guns in many more places than you can now. The difference is, fifty years ago there were no background checks, no waiting periods, no finger printing, no registration forms, no gun-free zones . . . and no outbreak of mass shootings. The legal requirements for purchasing a gun can be easily circumvented by a would-be killer. There will always be black-market guns available. If a criminal is fixated on committing a crime like murder, rape, or armed robbery, do you really think he will be swayed by a law restricting his possession of a firearm? Most of the recent mass killings actually happened in gun-free zones, probably because the killer knew there would be little, if any, resistance.

Gun-control proponents should redirect their efforts to the person using the gun, not the gun itself. Mental illness is the primary cause of mass murders. Unless you pass laws that address mental illness, you are wasting your time. Mass murderers who kill children, and their own relatives, are not likely to follow the regulations. Mass killings, as horrendous as they are, are only a tiny fraction of the murders being committed.

There are numerous reasons that better explain the overall murder rates: an increase in gang activity, the celebrity given to some killers, sensationalized violence within the entertainment industry, and proportionately light punishment for repeat violent offenders. In my opinion, those who commit crimes using a firearm, and repeat offenders, must be punished more severely. Gun owners should not be the ones being punished.

It can be argued that the most fundamental of all rights, is the right to defend one's self. Anti-gun advocates argue that guns are not designed to defend, they are designed to kill. Duh! If my wife, at 120 lbs., is attacked by a 300 lb. rapist, I want her to have the power to kill. There are times when the only way to stop evil is to kill it.

We need to promote responsible gun ownership, which includes education and training, and we need to help those who don't own guns understand that guns are simply a tool.

CHAPTER FIVE

Immigration

According to the Center For Immigration studies, the number of legal and illegal immigrants living in the U.S. reached an all-time record of 41.3 million people, as of July 2013. This estimate may actually be low, as the number of estimated illegal immigrants ranges from 11.5 million to more than twenty-five million.

The majority of Americans do not favor amnesty or increased immigration. A Gallup Poll taken in June 2014, showed that forty-one percent of adults in the U.S. want to see immigration decreased, while only twenty-two percent said they would like to see immigration increased.

There are strong ideological views on both sides of the argument. The far-left wants open borders and complete amnesty. The opinions of the Independents and Republicans are varied, but most want secure borders, a strict immigration plan, and a more business-friendly guest worker program.

Liberals state that America is a nation of immigrants and that it was immigrants who helped build this country, and because of this, we should welcome all immigrants. Part of that statement is true. Immigrants did help build this country. But the immigrants who came through Ellis Island were far different than those arriving today. The immigrants who came through Ellis Island did not get government assistance. There was no welfare state. They all brought important skills with them. These immigrants included those who were tailors, master carpenters, stone masons, bricklayers, artisans, and other working skills, all of which enhanced the American economy. They either made it on their own, or relied on family or friends until they could. About seventy percent of those immigrants were men in their prime. They learned English and adopted to American culture. They did not try to establish their prior culture in America. They were Americans first and foremost. They were screened for health issues and quarantined, if necessary. When the wars came, they fought for America, and they bled red, white, and blue.

In those early days of immigration, the immigrants came to America for a better life, knowing that the culture they were leaving was a failure. In the 1950s, half of all immigrants were from Europe. The Europeans eventually stopped immigrating to America, because Europe became more like America. By the 1970s, three-fourths were from Asia and Latin America.

Today, immigrants want to bring their cultures with them, along with those resulting socio-economic failures. Many current immigrants are only here for free healthcare and government assistance. According to Harvard economist George Borjas, welfare and other social programs are a magnet that draws non-working women, children, and the elderly—and keeps them here indefinitely. Many are low-skilled, under-educated, and have no desire to learn English or assimilate into our culture. Immigration today is a product of the Great Society, fueled by an entitlement mentality. In the first ten years after the Immigration and Nationality Act of 1965 was passed, immigration increased by sixty percent. Despite assurances from Edward Kennedy that America would not be adversely impacted, there have been a number of negative side-effects, including increased crime, overcrowded schools, increased healthcare costs, lower wages, higher insurance costs, higher taxes, voter fraud, and cultural degradation. Dozens of hospitals have had to close because immigrants with no insurance have exhausted the resources, lacking the ability to compensate for services received.

Currently, many other western nations are restricting immigration due to the same issues we are facing. We would be wise to do the same. The historical existence of immigration does not mean we can abandon our immigration laws.

In contrast to earlier immigrants, the percentage of skilled workers has dropped dramatically. Less than six percent of the legal immigrants in 2009 were admitted because they possessed skills which were deemed essential to the U.S. economy.

U.S. workers and immigrant workers are often competing for the same jobs. Studies that indicate differently are not based on actual observations of labor market conditions. The argument that immigrants are taking only the jobs that Americans don't want is false. America does not have a labor shortage, we have a job shortage. As such, a massive influx of illegal workers disproportionately harms low-skilled American workers. For every job occupied by an illegal immigrant, there is one legal resident who does not have that opportunity. A report by the Center for Immigration Studies, released in 2014, found that almost all of the net employment growth in the United States since 2000 has gone to immigrants, both legal and illegal. The report shows that 127,000 fewer working-age natives held jobs in the first quarter of 2014 than in 2000. In contrast, the number of immigrants with a job had increased by 5.7 million in the same period.

Potential workers in the U.S. currently include twenty-five million unemployed workers with a high school diploma, plus an additional 25.7 million with varying degrees of college education.

Republicans may someday attract a majority of Hispanic voters, but pandering to illegal immigrants and La Raza, the Hispanic civil-rights organization, will not accomplish anything. All you will end up with is an additional ten to twenty million low-skilled, low-wage, uninformed voters who prefer a bigger government that provides more assistance. Adding to an already bloated welfare state is not in anyone's best interest.

Immigration is not a major concern within the Latino community. A survey of Latino voters in 2014, commissioned by Univision, found that education was the number one issue for Latinos, followed by jobs, government spending, social security, government impact on personal finances, health care, immigration, and crime. Only eight percent listed immigration as a priority issue. Fifty-three percent of those surveyed supported secure borders *prior* to providing a pathway to citizenship for illegals. This survey was done in California. The Latino voters in the rest of the country are likely to take an even more conservative stance.

There will always be a portion of the Hispanic constituency whose values and beliefs lead them to be conservative. However, recent studies have indicated that an increasingly larger percentage of Hispanics are becoming dependent on government, and that they are abandoning traditional values.

Job creation, fiscal responsibility, and a well-articulated conservative message, will appeal to far more Hispanic voters than politicians dressed as Santa Claus.

The American National Election Study found that eighty-five percent of Hispanics felt that strong government involvement was needed to handle economic problems. With that degree of support for bigger government, and a majority who receive direct and means-tested benefits, it is doubtful that a majority will ever vote Republican. Passage of an amnesty bill would virtually eliminate any chance of Republicans getting a majority of the Hispanic vote in the future.

Having spent a great deal of time in Mexico, I have developed a deep appreciation for the Mexican people and their traditional culture. Unfortunately, many of the immigrants coming from Mexico, and other parts of Latin America, are not representative of the Mexican people I came to know and love. It would be wonderful if we could open the borders without any fiscal impact, or worries about increasing crime, disease, or terrorism threats. It would be great if every immigrant was eventually able to make a positive contribution to our economy, without jeopardizing the employment of a single American worker. It would be even better if all immigrants wanted to be Americans, learn our language, and not try to change the core of American traditionalism. But, that is not the case. Along with many immigrants that I would eagerly welcome, there are many who come at a huge price, on many levels. Let me give you some examples.

The Cost of Immigration

A recent study by the Heritage Foundation found that the average household headed by an illegal immigrant with a high-school education receives about $24,721 in government benefits and services, while only paying about $10,334 in taxes, for a net fiscal deficit of $14,387 per household. Those households headed by an illegal immigrant without a high school diploma, receive $20,485 more in benefits and services per year than they pay in taxes.

A report released in June 2011 by the Migration Policy Institute, showed that sixty-two percent of Mexican immigrants over the age of twenty-five do not have a high school diploma. At virtually every stage of their lifetime, the average illegal immigrant will produce a net fiscal deficit.

Even lawful immigrant households are an economic drain. Lawful immigrant households receive significantly more government assistance, on average, than native U.S. households.

Legal immigrants without a high school diploma actually qualify for even more benefits, including Social Security Retirement, but pay only an average of about $4,400 in additional taxes per year. This equates to a net tax deficit of $36,993.00.

There are four primary types of benefits that government provides for low-income individuals:

- Direct Benefits

- Means-tested welfare benefits

- Public education

- Population-based services

Direct benefits include Unemployment Compensation, Workers Compensation, Social Security and Medicare.

Means-tested welfare benefits include more than eighty government programs such as Food Stamps, Medicaid, Housing Assistance, Temporary Assistance for Needy Families, Supplemental Security Income, and Earned Income Tax Credits.

The cost of public education averages about $12,300 per student per year per household, but is often free or subsidized for low-income families. Costs can be more for immigrant students needing lunch subsidies or bilingual assistance.

Population-based services are those that are provided to the general populace, such as Police, Fire, Public Parks, Highway Maintenance, etc.

The average U.S. household received $31,585 worth of these benefits in 2010.

In contrast, the average U.S. household headed by a person who is college-educated, paid $29,250 more in taxes than they received in government benefits, and legal immigrants with a college degree paid an average of about $24,000 more in taxes than benefits and services received.

Amnesty would increase the average annual tax deficit by fifty-five percent for former illegal immigrants , while allowing them access to more than eighty means-tested welfare programs. Once amnesty has been fully implemented, the average benefits and services to former illegal immigrant households would increase to about $43,900, with taxes paid only being about $16,000 per year, for a fiscal deficit of $27,900 per year per household. If amnesty is enacted, the average illegal immigrant would receive about $582,000 more in benefits and services over his lifetime than he pays in taxes, based on 2010 dollars. Amnesty would also result in increased retirement costs. There would be an estimated net fiscal deficit of $22,700 per retired amnesty recipient per year for Social Security and Medicare, putting additional strain on already overburdened programs.

Proponents of amnesty argue it would help make Social Security solvent, because the illegal immigrants would pay more in FICA taxes after amnesty. However, based on present earnings, the average illegal immigrant would only be paying about $3,700 per year in FICA taxes while receiving net benefits of about $25,000 per year. How does that equate to a fiscal positive?

The Heritage Foundation estimates the national fiscal deficit for illegal immigrant labor to be about $55 billion. The Federation of Americans for Immigration Reform estimates the deficit is approximately $99 billion.

A study by Stanford professors Michael Boskin and John Cogan, found that from the mid- 1980s to 2005, California's population grew by about ten million. During that same period, Medicaid recipients increased by a whopping seven million, while tax filers, who actually paid taxes, only increased by 150,000. At the same time, the prison population in California rose by 115,000. In 2009, the estimated cost of incarcerating a criminal alien in California was $34,448 annually. This is not the model we want to replicate on a national scale.

According to a report by the Treasury Department's inspector general, illegal immigrants fraudulently received $4.2 billion in child-support tax credits in 2010, increasing to an estimated $7.4 billion in 2012.

Another story that is seldom reported is the burden which illegal immigrants put on hospitals. Under the Emergency Medical Treatment and Active Labor Act of 1985 (EMTALA), emergency rooms must care for uninsured people regardless of ability or intent to pay. Virtually any condition, including headaches, coughs, and hangnails can be labeled as an "emergency" under this act. This degradation of the medical system, and subsequent non-payment for services, has already forced more than eighty California hospitals to close their doors—and that's only taking California into account.

More than 60,000 unaccompanied immigrant children arrived in the U.S. in 2014. That is ten times higher than 2011 levels, and is expected to cost U.S. taxpayers an additional $2 billion.

A welfare state is not compatible with mass immigration. It is fiscally irresponsible to continue to allow low-skilled, poorly educated immigrants, both legal and illegal into this country. The costs are unsustainable. With few exceptions, our government should limit immigration to only those who will be net fiscal contributors.

The Criminal Side of Immigration

The main stream media calls illegal immigration a "victimless crime." It is true that most illegal aliens' only crime is breaking immigration laws. However, a disproportionately large percentage of illegal aliens *are* criminals and sexual predators.

Other crimes that illegal alien criminals are commonly involved in include drug trafficking, various types of fraud, robbery, prostitution, assault, and burglary. We should not be afraid to address the issue of crime by illegals, out of fear of upsetting the immigrant population, because many of those within the immigrant population are actually victims.

In 1980, there were fewer than 9,000 criminal aliens in our state and federal prisons. As of 2009, there were 295,959 criminal

aliens incarcerated in state prisons and local jails in the U.S.—
204,136 in local jails and 91,823 in state prisons. An additional
55,000 were incarcerated in federal prisons.

In 2009, criminal aliens from Mexico made up sixty-six percent of
all illegals incarcerated in state prisons, and another nine percent
were from Honduras, Guatemala, and El Salvador.

In 2009, criminal aliens from Mexico made up seventy percent of
all illegals in local jails, with Honduras, Guatemala, and El Salvador
adding an additional eleven percent.

At that time, the cost per individual to incarcerate a criminal alien
was $34,448 per year in California, and $29,523 per year in New
York. The average cost nationwide was $12,520 per year.

A study done by the GAO sampled approximately 249,000 criminal
aliens, arrested between August 1955 and April 2010. About
ninety percent of the arrests in the study occurred after 1990.
This study group was arrested for a total of 2.9 million offenses, or
about 11.6 offenses per criminal alien. At ninety percent, an
average of more than 136,000 offenses were committed each
year since 1990. Using the same ninety percent calculation, during
the same period from 1990 to 2010, this group alone committed
approximately 191,000 assaults, 103,000 burglaries, 85,000
weapons violations, 63,000 sex offenses, 22,500 murders, and
13,000 kidnappings. And that is just this study group. Given the
increase in illegal aliens since 2009, and the relatively small
sampling size, the true numbers are obviously much higher.

From 2008 to 2012, 143,000 criminal aliens were arrested and
jailed in Texas alone. They were charged with 447,000 offenses,
including more than 5,000 rapes and 2,000 murders. That's in one
state.

An in-depth study done by the Violent Crimes Institute, covering
the period from January 1999 through April 2006, arrived at a
conservative estimate of 240,000 illegal immigrant sex offenders
in the U.S. over the course of that time. Of the 1500 sex offenders

in the study, each averaged four victims. The crimes committed included rape, sexual homicides, and child molestation. Eighty-two percent of the victims were known to their attacker. Forty-seven percent of the child molestation victims were Hispanic. The average age of molestation victims was six. The offenders typically had access to the victims after working as a day laborer at or near the victim's homes. Twenty-two percent of the sex crimes committed by illegal immigrants targeted victims with mental or physical disabilities. Approximately sixty-three percent of the offenders had been deported at least once before.

Based on that study, there were an estimated 960,000 sex crimes committed by illegal aliens throughout the U.S. during that eighty-eight month period. That equates to 363 sex crimes per day.

In April 2005, the GAO released a report based on the study of 55,322 illegal aliens incarcerated during 2003. They found the illegal aliens in the study had been arrested an average of eight times each. Ninety percent had previously been arrested, fifty percent of those had been arrested for a violent crime or drug-related felony.

If criminal aliens have continued to average eight arrests, then as of 2010, the number of incarcerated illegal aliens (351,000) represents more than 2.8 million crimes. Do you still think illegal immigration is a "victimless crime?" Keep in mind, these are only the criminals who have been arrested.

In 2011, there were approximately 8800 gang-related deaths in the U.S. The National Youth Gang Survey Analysis found that total gang members in the U.S. are forty-nine percent Hispanic, a large percentage of which are illegal. As a result of inadequate border security, known gang members, including members of Mara Salvatrucha (MS-13), are easily crossing into the United States. Texas alone is estimated to have more than 100,000 gang members who are illegals.

If I haven't yet given you enough reason to secure the border, consider the following. Between 2005 and 2011, U.S. Border

Patrol agents along the U.S.-Mexico border, seized 72,000 pounds of cocaine, 13.2 million pounds of marijuana, 4,700 pounds of methamphetamine, and 1,400 pounds of heroin. This constitutes only an estimated ten percent of the drugs that actually made it into the U.S. At a street value of $2000 per uncut ounce, the cocaine that made it through would have a street value of more than $20 billion.

And then there is terrorism. A report released in March 2010, by the Department of Justice National Security Division, showed that international terrorism investigations had led to the convictions of 399 individuals since September 11, 2001. Of these, 173 individuals were aliens in the U.S. with or without legal immigration status.

In September 2014, several agencies reported that members of the Islamic State (ISIS) were operating in Cuidad Juarez, Mexico, just across the border from El Paso, Texas. Immigration officials indicate there is a very serious ISIS threat, and it is likely that ISIS members have already, or will soon, come across the border into the U.S.

Aside from inadequate border security, approximately five million immigrants in the U.S. are here in violation of temporary visas. Many of those who have overstayed their visas are from countries with known ties to terrorism.

"Sanctuary Laws" may actually aid terrorists by offering them a safe haven in cities like San Francisco, Houston, and Los Angeles.

Now comes the most disturbing problem of all. Under current policies, the deportation of even those criminals who are violent can be terminated based on political considerations, family relationships, support of advocacy groups, and several other factors. Public safety does not appear to be a serious consideration.

In August 2012, the Congressional Research Service released a report which found that between October 2008 and July 2011,

159,286 legal and illegal aliens were arrested and eventually released back onto the streets. A total of 7,283 illegal aliens, who should have been deported, were later charged with a total of 16,226 crimes, including nineteen murders, and 142 sex crimes (including rape and child molestation). They were also charged with almost 1,000 other major criminal offenses.

Almost three-fourths of the aliens who were detained by U.S. Immigration and Customs Enforcement (ICE) in 2013 had criminal or immigration *convictions* so serious that detention was *required* by statute. Yet, based on a report from the Center for Immigration Studies, ICE officials released 36,007 convicted criminal aliens from custody in 2013 alone. Those were criminals who had been incarcerated for a variety of offenses, including murder, kidnapping, sexual assault, and aggravated assault.

A recently released report from the Department of Homeland Security Inspector General shows that hundreds more violent criminal aliens have been released since 2013.

Some ICE agents have been disciplined for upholding the law. How's that for border security?

Illegal Immigration and Disease

Most legal immigrants are screened for infectious diseases and treated if necessary. But, Illegal aliens don't undergo health screenings like those required of legal immigrants. Many illegal aliens cross the border to get treated for existing diseases that can be transmitted to others along the way. Many of the diseases are types which don't immediately show symptoms, so illegal immigrants with these diseases are going all over the U.S. before the diseases are diagnosed, exposing thousands of people.

Beginning in early 2014, thousands of unaccompanied illegal alien children began flooding across the southern U.S. border. The children were not only allowed into the U.S., they were given safe haven at Department of Homeland Security (DHS) holding facilities, and relocated to cities all over the United States. In most instances, officials and citizens of these respective states and cities were never notified.

Many of these children had infectious diseases. In June 2014, there were reported outbreaks of scabies, chicken pox, MRSA staff infections, and drug-resistant tuberculosis at several of the holding facilities. Scabies was even contracted by some of the border patrol agents. The only thing separating the sick from the healthy at the DHS Holding Facilities housing the illegal children was a strip of yellow police caution tape. Unvaccinated children with diseases coming from third-world countries will likely infect many unvaccinated American children, as well as other children in their respective holding facilities.

In July 2014, Todd Starnes of *Fox News* reported there were three confirmed cases of tuberculosis at the holding facility in Austin, Texas, as well as many more children showing symptoms of T.B. at several other facilities. He also reported cases of chicken pox, and said some children had "lice so severe they can be seen crawling down the faces of the children."

The DHS is denying all requests for interviews with the doctors and medical staff who are treating the sick immigrants, and the facilities are heavily secured. This is not what you would expect from a holding facility for children. Obviously, there is some degree of a cover-up. Could it be that they are concerned an outbreak of a serious disease would all but destroy their immigration narrative? I would think the well-being of our citizens would come first.

The disease problem did not start with these children—they just helped magnify the problem. As immigration has increased over the last few decades, we have seen outbreaks of diseases in America which used to be confined to third-world countries. Look at some of the diseases that are now in the U.S.

Malaria

In 2011, the number of malaria cases hit a forty-year high, up fourteen percent from 2010, which was also up fourteen percent from 2009. Eighteen people died from malaria in those three years.

Tuberculosis

There is now a drug-resistant strain that is highly infectious which has previously not been an issue.

Dengue Fever

As of September 2014, there were 1,060,441 cases in the Americas, mostly in Central and South America. There are now 172 confirmed cases in the U.S., all but two of which have been classified as "imported."

West Nile Virus

West Nile Virus did not exist in the U.S. until 1999. Through 2013, there have been 39,557 reported cases with 1,668 fatalities.

Chagas Disease

Chagas is generally contracted through contact with the feces of an infected triatomine bug, a blood-sucking insect that feeds on humans and animals. An estimated eight-million people are infected with Chagas throughout Mexico, Central America, and South America. The CDC estimates that more than 300,000 persons with Chagas live in the U.S., most of which acquired their infections in endemic countries.

Leprosy

Leprosy had been slowly fading in the United States in recent decades. In 1980, there were 456 new cases of leprosy reported in the U.S. By 2000, the number of new cases had dropped to seventy-seven. In 2009, the last year for which the CDC has data, the number of leprosy cases had increased to 213, an increase of

276 percent. During the ten-year period ending in 2009, Texas reported 225 new cases of leprosy, and California reported 235 new cases.

In the first seven months of 2014, seventy-one illegal aliens from Ebola-affected West African countries were apprehended at the U.S.-Mexico border. These are only the ones who were caught, and likely only represent a portion of the total who were not caught. The incubation period for Ebola is up to twenty-one days, which would give illegals plenty of time to cross the border and assimilate into the population.

Jobs and Illegal Immigrants

American workers lose an estimated $405 billion due to companies using lower-cost legal and illegal foreign workers. This equates to an average of about $2800 lost per American worker per year. Studies show that low-wage immigrant workers drive down the wages of native-born workers, including Hispanics born in this country.

The immigrants who came to America in the early 1900s had skills equal to, or superior to, most of the existing workers in America at that time. The majority of immigrants today have little or no training in most blue-collar occupations, and only a small percentage of immigrant worker admissions are based on skill levels or education criteria.

Big corporations are lobbying for amnesty under the guise that they need more high-tech professionals in the STEM disciplines (Science, Technology, Engineering, Mathematics), due to a shortage of such workers in the U.S. In reality, they are looking for cheaper labor. There is no shortage of STEM workers in the U.S., there is, in fact, a huge surplus. About fifteen million U.S. residents have at least a B.A. in a STEM discipline, however 11.4 million of them are not employed in a STEM occupation. The Economic Policy Institute also finds that there is "more than a sufficient supply of workers available to work in STEM occupations." A Rand Corporation study in 2004 stated there was no evidence that a shortage has existed since 1990.

A study done by the Pew Hispanic Center found that, of the Mexican immigrants who have been in the U.S. for less than two years, only five percent had been unemployed in Mexico.

In the 1960s, President Kennedy ended a guest-worker program that had been in existence for more than two decades, a program which allowed 45,000 Mexican laborers to cross the border to harvest tomatoes in California. At the time, they were harvesting about 2.2 million tons of tomatoes. The farmers quickly automated, and began using mechanical tomato-picking equipment. Decades later, that equipment is still in use, harvesting twelve million tons of tomatoes with only 5,000 workers. The farmers proved that there was a more efficient way to harvest through automation, and the resulting increases in costs to the consumer were minimal.

Agricultural economists have estimated that without illegal farm workers, the retail cost of fresh produce would only increase by about three percent in the summer-fall season, and less than two percent in the winter-spring season. Plus, a reduction in the illegal immigrant population would result in higher wages and better working conditions for native workers.

In Their Own Words

"This [estimate] translates to 93 sex offenders and 12 serial sexual offenders coming across U.S. borders illegally per day." Deborah Scherman-Kauflin, Violent Crimes Institute, Atlanta

"They're all contagious. So now we're transporting people into different parts of the state, different parts of the country, and some of these viruses are asymptomatic at this point—they're showing no symptoms." Border Patrol Agent Chris Cabrera

"It's one giant emergency room. They tell me tuberculosis has become a very dangerous issue there. Nurses say the number of children representing symptoms of tuberculosis is 'simply staggering.' Spitting up blood, chest pains, constant coughing. There are at least three confirmed cases for the illegals in Austin, Texas. The federal government is covering up the threat of the health crises. They say the kids have Scabies. They also say they have Chicken Pox, and lice so severe they can be seen crawling down the faces of the children." Todd Starnes, *Fox News*

"As criminal aliens are released to the streets and ICE instead takes disciplinary action against its own officers for making lawful arrests, it appears clear that federal law enforcement officers are the enemy and not those that break our nation's laws." Chris Crane, president National ICE Council

"This growing wave [of immigrants] threatens Israelis' jobs, is changing the character of the country, and we must stop it." Israel PM Benjamin Netanyahu speaking on illegal immigration in Israel

"In scores of our cities and market towns, this country, in a short space of time, has frankly become unrecognizable." Nigel Farage, Leader of UKIP, speaking on mass immigration in Britain

"Multiculturalism 'opposes the idea of a common culture, rejects the goals of assimilation and integration, and celebrates the immutability of diverse and separate racial and ethnic communities.'" Arthur Schlesinger

Conclusion

Immigration policies should serve the best interests of the American people, and we need to be selective in how the policy is applied. We need to seal the border, first and foremost. Then, emphasis should be placed on economic growth, national security, and the well-being of the American public.

These policies should not be shaped by advocacy groups who want to turn immigration into the next civil-rights movement. Nor should we be swayed by businesses interested only in cheap labor. We need to follow the lead of other western nations by allowing only workers who have skills that are in demand or education beyond a high school level, who speak English, and who have the best chance of assimilating into our society.

Immigration only makes sense if it's done in a responsible manner, allowing those who will have a positive impact, and excluding those with criminal records, infectious diseases, or those who will be a negative economic contributor. Mass immigration comes with many unwanted side-effects, such as increased crime, disease, cultural degradation, and an increased burden on government benefits and services. As such, many western nations are restricting immigration. Great Britain, France, Italy, Norway, Switzerland, and Israel all have very restrictive immigration policies, which are vigorously enforced.

A Pew Research Poll found that sixty-four percent of Italians see immigration as a "very big problem."

The Swiss want strict limits on immigration in order to maintain their national identity.

A spike in violent crime led Israel to tighten its immigration laws.

In Britain, the leader of UKIP, the most popular political party, is recommending a five-year moratorium on immigration, due to the dramatic negative changes in many cities. Many English neighborhoods have become Islamic enclaves, with increasing crime and no semblance of British culture.

All of those other western nations have experienced the same problems associated with mass immigration that we are dealing with, and have taken steps to stop it. That is the sensible thing to do. How long will American politicians continue to compromise the well-being of its citizens for no other reason than to secure a voting base?

Unskilled and low-skilled immigrants add little to our economy, but come at a great cost. The average immigrant, lacking the skills needed to succeed in a modern economy, will receive far more than they will ever pay. Those with little or no education face a lifetime of economic disadvantage and government dependency. The problem is magnified if they do not speak English. Granting them legal status won't change the fact that they are not equipped to be successful in the U.S.

When we bring in labor from other countries, we aren't simply bringing in workers. We are bringing in differing cultures, politics, languages, belief systems, religions, preferences, etc. It's much more complicated than it seems initially.

Unlike immigrants of the early 1900s, many immigrants who come to the U.S. today have no intention of adopting our culture or giving up their socialistic beliefs. Many maintain loyalty to their home countries, while using the U.S. for employment, free healthcare, and government assistance. As a result, the U.S. will slowly start to morph into the failed culture they were so anxious to leave. Our focus on multiculturalism actually encourages immigrants NOT to assimilate into the American culture. What's worse is that immigrants who are already poor are now taught they are victims of income inequality and racial inequality, and encouraged to espouse historical ethnic grievances. The result is a lot of anti-Americans living in America.

Rewarding people who break the law encourages other people to break the law. You end up with a never-ending cycle of illegal entry and amnesty, as the stability of our country continues to be compromised.

Those on the Left seem to be more interested in votes than for the well-being of the average American citizen. For them, this is about building a permanent progressive majority—at the expense of American workers and taxpayers, including legal immigrants.

CHAPTER SIX

Minimum Wage

Since its inception in 1938 , the federal minimum wage has been increased twenty-four times. Yet we still have poverty and income inequality. Why? Because raising the minimum wage has been proven to be completely ineffective at reducing poverty. Studies over the last seventy-five years, however, do show raising the minimum wage is effective at reducing employment. Minimum wage increases have accounted for millions of lost jobs. The topic of wage increases has also become a divisive political tool. It's one of those "feel good" issues that people equate with compassion for the poor—until they learn the truth.

There is nothing compassionate about taking someone's job away.

The very people we are told will benefit are the ones who ultimately get hurt the most: usually unskilled workers, immigrants and the disabled. Those who stand to gain the most from a minimum-wage increase are unions and politicians.

This chapter will expose not only the dismal track record of the minimum wage, but also the factors that will continue to make wage increase laws bad law for our future.

Once we understand the facts, it is difficult to argue in favor of a minimum wage increase. Those politicians who are lobbying against the minimum wage are often seen as being insensitive to the plight of the working-class poor. Most mainstream news organizations continue to perpetuate that narrative. The anti-minimum wage politicians are actually the ones who care enough about their constituents to stand up and fight for their best interests. Eventually, they will be vindicated, as more of this information becomes common knowledge.

The mainstream media has become a mouthpiece for the Democratic Party and continues to report its news accordingly. The minimum wage issue is no exception. Numerous news outlets recently published headlines that read "Gallup Poll Shows 76% Support Minimum Wage Increase." Remember, polls can be deceptive. What the mainstream media didn't tell you is that the question Gallup asked was "Would you vote for a law which raised the Federal minimum wage to $9.00 per hour?. " The Gallup polling staff never mentioned any of the adverse effects of a minimum wage increase to the respondents.

A Reason-Rupe poll, taken about the same time, showed virtually identical results when asked the same question. Then they asked the same respondents if they would vote for the minimum wage increase if they knew a number of people would lose their jobs. This time fifty-seven percent opposed the increase and only thirty-eight percent said they would vote for it. The percentage opposed would be even higher if the respondents knew the entire minimum-wage story.

Advocates for a minimum-wage increase cite several reasons for their support: 1) to provide a "living wage" that better reflects the cost of living, 2) to lift people out of poverty and 3) to narrow the income-inequality gap. Let's take a look at these reasons individually.

Living Wage Versus Learning Wage

The minimum wage is often more aptly referred to as a "learning wage." The importance of a minimum-wage job is to provide skills and training, which in turn makes employees more productive and gives them the ability to command higher pay in the future. Nearly two-thirds of minimum-wage workers receive a pay increase within one year. That raise, for full-time workers averages about fourteen percent. Although there are some people who are older head-of-households working full-time for minimum wage, that is the exception. Minimum-wage earners are generally new to the job market, often teenagers with little or no skills, immigrants, unskilled older workers, workers with disabilities, and people without a high-school diploma. Over half of the people in America started their careers making within a dollar of the minimum wage. Those who started higher usually had additional education beyond high school. Almost sixty percent of minimum-wage workers have no more than a high-school education.

According to the Bureau of Labor Statistics, there were approximately 144-million people employed in the United States in 2013. Only 2.3 percent of these workers earned at or below minimum wage (approximately 3.3 million workers). Of this group, just over half (50.4 percent or 1.663 million) were only twenty-four years of age or younger. Another 13.2 percent (436,000) were between 25-29 years of age. Workers over the age of thirty making minimum wage only accounted for 0.8 percent of the total U.S. workforce. More than two-thirds work part-time, and approximately half work in the food-service industry. Another 468,000 worked in the retail industry, in which most of the jobs are generally entry-level. The majority of these minimum-wage earners were teenagers and young adults living with their parents.

The average "family" income for these households was $53,000 per year. Two-thirds lived in families with incomes that were over 150 percent of the poverty mark. Also, keep in mind the numbers shown above do not include additional income such as overtime, tips, or commissions. Obviously, those needing a "living wage" only accounted for a small percentage of the minimum-wage earners. The family with a single parent working full-time at minimum wage—which Democrats often cite as being a major issue—accounts for only four percent of minimum-wage workers (approximately 132,000). Most of these single parent families would be better off without the minimum-wage increase, as you will learn in the next section.

Minimum Wage Versus Poverty

The president claims that raising the minimum wage from $7.25 per hour to $10.10 per hour will lift a million full-time minimum-wage workers out of poverty. I hate to bust anybody's bubble, but they are already out of poverty. A person who makes the current minimum wage of $7.25 per hour will make $15,080 per year working full-time, which is $3,410 over the poverty limit. Their hourly wage does not include tips, overtime, or commissions. This same individual will also get a tax credit of 9.2% or $1,387 for an effective minimum wage of $7.91 per hour. But wait . . . there's more. According to the CBO, the average person in this scenario would also qualify for up to $22,700 in government assistance. If the full amount of assistance is added, the effective minimum wage jumps to $18.83 per hour. Once you raise the minimum wage, those benefits will start to disappear.

A CBO report issued in 2012 found that a single parent with one child, earning between $15,000 and $25,000 annually, experiences almost no financial benefit from a wage increase up to $25,000. What is gained in wages is lost through reduced benefits. For example, a low-income worker who receives a wage increase could lose all or part of the following: SNAP benefits, WIC benefits, child-care subsidies, housing vouchers, Medicaid benefits, CHIP benefits, insurance subsidies, and all or part of their

Earned Income Tax Credit. On top of that, they would then pay additional payroll and income taxes.

There have been eight studies done since 1995 that examined the impact of minimum-wage increases on poverty. All but one found that prior minimum-wage increases had no effect on poverty. These same studies also concluded that while some poverty-level, low-skilled workers did see an increase in income, many other low-skilled workers either lost their job or suffered a reduction in hours, leading to reduced income which resulted in increased poverty.

Even if there were no negative effects of a minimum-wage increase, relatively few people would benefit. During the last minimum-wage increase (up to $7.25/hour), only 15.8 percent of the workers who benefited from the increase lived in poor households. Few people who live in poverty work at a minimum-wage job. Over sixty-three percent have no job at all. Raising the minimum wage will likely hurt those in poverty the most. The minimum-wage workers who live in poverty are generally over twenty-five-years old. If a person is over twenty-five and still making minimum wage in a job that has no tips, commissions, or overtime, then it is likely that there is an issue with skill level and/or productivity. These are the ones who stand the greatest chance of losing their jobs, or being priced out of the job market altogether. While an increase in minimum wage will pull some families out of poverty, a proportionate amount of workers will lose their jobs and fall *into* poverty. The only real solution to reducing poverty is through job creation.

The Minimum Wage and Income Inequality

The "real" income of the lowest wage earners in America, compared to the highest wage earners, has been grossly misrepresented by the media. I discuss this later in this book, in more detail, in my chapter on income inequality.

In short, the media uses U.S. Census Bureau figures to arrive at their "facts" with regard to income inequality between the highest and lowest income quintiles. These figures are misleading for a number of reasons.

First, the Census Bureau bases their figures on household income, not individual income. The average number of working family members in the highest quintile is almost five times higher than the lowest quintile. This not only distorts the number of people in each quintile, it also distorts the income per capita.

Secondly, the Census Bureau uses what it calls "money income" in their calculations, which excludes important income variables such as government assistance payments, taxes, employee benefits, work hours, earned income credits, and other additional income sources. When these factors are taken into account, the income gap narrows substantially. Using all of the available income sources and tax liabilities, and adjusting for average hours worked, the income ratio between the highest quintile and the lowest quintile drops from the reported ratio of about $14.00 to each $1.00, to just over $3.00 to each $1.00. Obviously, that's not much of an income disparity. You will never see these numbers in the mainstream media.

The Minimum-Wage Track Record

There are few, if any, studies that provide convincing evidence of positive employment effects from having a mandated minimum-wage , increased or not. The positive minimum-wage studies often use monopsony models (one buyer in a market with many sellers) or institutional models (large entities that buy in volume) to explain the positive effects. However, most economists feel that these models are unrealistic in determining large-scale economic trends with regard to minimum wage. Studies based on competitive models (many buyers and many sellers) are most often used, as they reflect a more accurate picture of the current economic climate.

The primary finding of studies done since the minimum wage was first established, is that minimum-wage increases tend to reduce employment. The findings also show that the higher the minimum-wage increase, relative to competitive-market wage levels, the greater the loss of employment. The employment losses were found to disproportionately impact the least-skilled and most disadvantaged workers, including the disabled, immigrants, youth, unskilled workers and ethnic minorities. These workers were often replaced with higher-skilled workers whose production level helped restore previous profit margins. In this scenario, history will not show a net job loss, but once again the people who are most affected are the ones who can least afford it.

In a struggling economy, employers will not hire workers whose production level is below the wages being paid. If the minimum wage is raised to $10.10 per hour, then those workers whose labor brings in less than that to the business are no longer a good investment. As a result, young and unskilled workers will find fewer job opportunities as employers weigh the cost effectiveness of longer training periods to get them to a point of positive return. If you add the mandated cost of the Affordable Care Act, along with employer-paid taxes, to the proposed minimum-wage increase, the cost to an employer jumps to $12.71 per hour for a minimum-wage employee. It is more likely that an employer will operate with a reduced workforce or hire workers with stronger skill sets. The long-term effects will also be greater as businesses find alternative labor-saving methods of production through automation and mechanization.

Economists have estimated that a ten percent increase in labor costs will result in a workforce reduction of about three percent. If that statement holds true, then the current proposed minimum-wage hike (39.3%) would equate to a workforce reduction of at least twelve percent of those making minimum wage. Studies have also found that a ten percent minimum-wage increase would raise food prices by up to four percent. These effects are magnified during periods of sluggish economic conditions. Businesses have to adjust to any added costs of producing their goods or services. When labor costs increase, especially during rough economic periods, the business is left with few alternatives. They have the choice of cutting employee hours, reducing the number of employees, charging higher prices, or in the case of some larger businesses, automating jobs.

Proponents of minimum-wage increases argue that it should be done at the expense of the employer's profits. This is done quite often in the fast-food industry. However, most employers can't afford a reduction in profit margin, and usually face serious competition that would cause them to lose sales if prices were increased. This is especially true in a global economy. As a result of higher taxes, government regulations, and other increasing overhead costs, profit margins have already been diminished. Most of the businesses that employ minimum-wage workers are small businesses. A minimum-wage increase of any significance will result in numerous business failures and fewer new business starts. Overall, there is no economic gain. There is simply a redistribution of costs, with the greatest burden falling upon the employers, the unskilled workers and the consumers.

A Bit of Minimum-Wage History

More than two decades before the first minimum-wage law was passed , it was being discussed by two very prominent economic figures from different countries. But, it was not being discussed for the reasons you might think. Sidney Webb, a British economist and co-founder of the London School of Economics, and Royal Meeker, the Commissioner of Labor under Woodrow Wilson, both envisioned a minimum-wage mandate, along with other market interventions, as a potential means of keeping the lowest working class out of the workforce. They felt that a minimum wage would help weed out those too stupid or lazy to compete in a market economy, in particular, women, immigrants, and blacks. It is no surprise that they both were also early advocates of eugenics.

The first federal minimum wage was signed into law as part of the Fair Labor Standards Act on June 25, 1938. The original minimum wage was twenty-five cents per hour and it covered only about thirty-eight percent of the workforce, as compared to about eighty-five percent today. The result of that first minimum wage was job losses that numbered between 30,000 and 50,000 in the United States. Within a year of its implementation, an estimated 120,000 workers lost their jobs in Puerto Rico, which was also required to follow the new law. The Puerto Rican unemployment rate reached nearly fifty percent, nothing short of a disaster. Subsequent minimum-wage increases have continued to cause job losses, now numbering in the millions. The CBO report on the most recent minimum-wage proposal states that as many as one million jobs could be lost with this increase alone.

A more recent minimum-wage disaster, that you probably didn't read about, happened in American Samoa starting in 2007. This was a classic example of a well-intentioned government mandate being implemented despite opposition from those it was intended to "benefit".

American Samoa is a small chain of islands in the south pacific that has been an American territory since the turn of the twentieth century. It has a small economy and considerably lower average incomes than that of the United States. In 2007, the tuna canning industry constituted a significant portion of Samoa's private sector job market. At that time, the minimum wage in Samoa was $3.26 compared to $5.15 in the United States. On May 25th of that year, Congress passed the Fair Minimum Wage Act of 2007, which increased the federal minimum wage in the U.S. from $5.15 to $7.25 in three increments ($5.85 per hour as of 7/24/07, $6.55 per hour as of 7/24/08, and $7.25 per hour as of 7/24/09). Despite objections from Samoa's Representative, the act also mandated that the minimum wage be increased in American Samoa at a rate of $.50 per year until it reached the same level as the United States. By the time the third increase took effect (to $4.76 per hour), employment in American Samoa had fallen fourteen percent and inflation-adjusted wages had fallen eleven percent (average earnings increased by about five percent, but local consumer prices rose by almost twenty percent). Between the two major tuna canneries, Starkist and Chicken of The Sea, a total of about 3000 jobs were lost. Chicken of The Sea closed its canning facilities and outsourced it's jobs to Thailand. Starkist laid off workers, cut hours and benefits, and instituted a hiring freeze. The unemployment rate jumped to more than thirty-five percent. By contrast, Switzerland, which has no minimum wage, was at three percent unemployment.

American Samoa lost the freedom to manage its own labor market. Well meaning bureaucrats imposed their will on the Samoan people and set artificial wage floors that the local economy could not support. The basic economic law of supply and demand was ignored at the expense of the Samoan people.

Common Sense

A little bit of logic will go a long way in the discussion of a minimum wage. There are some questions which no one in the Democrat party has been able to provide a satisfactory answer to. The first question is," How did you arrive at a figure of $10.10 for the federal minimum wage?" The answer is that it is a totally arbitrary figure. There is no economic data that supports that amount. Any universal minimum wage will adversely affect most of the country. The same minimum wage used in Florida is likely to be too high for Idaho and too low for New York. There is no way it can be adequate in every market in the country due to the large disparity in the cost of living from one state to another , or even one city to another. Even when individual states have raised minimum wages based on their unique economic conditions, research has still shown that a higher minimum wage will reduce employment for less-skilled workers. A decision that potentially risks a million jobs should warrant some degree of historical economic data support.

Another question I have has two parts; 1) "Why didn't the president and Congress just raise the minimum wage to $10.10 in 2009 or 2010 when the Democrats had control of all three branches of government?" and 2) Why are the Democrats making this a top priority now , when there has barely been an issue in the last five years?" The reasons are very simple. First of all, the Democrats know it's a job killer. They only bring this issue up to be used as a deflection from other issues (Obamacare, IRS scandal, NSA scandal, etc.) , and as a device to perpetuate the belief that politicians who are against a minimum wage are insensitive to the needs of the working poor. Unfortunately, there are millions of voters who are oblivious to the facts of most political issues, and most of the media outlets are a poor conduit to their education.

I am also curious as to why a party that finds minimum wage rates to be such an important issue would also support increased immigration levels. The two seem to be counterproductive. An example would be the Immigration and Nationality Act of 1965, which has allowed millions of unskilled workers to flood the U.S., driving down demand, and ultimately the cost of labor. The buying power of the dollar was continuing to make significant gains from 1938 until it peaked in 1968 , at which point the effects of the Hart-Celler Act (Immigration and Nationality Act) appears to have reversed the trend. As a result, the dollar's buying power has seen a dramatic overall drop.

Who Benefits From a Minimum-Wage Increase

The preponderance of evidence has proven that minimum-wage laws are harmful to low-skilled workers, youth, immigrants, the disabled, and the economy in general. So who is it that does benefit from an increase in the minimum wage? The answer:

unions and Democrats. Have you ever wondered why unions always come out in enthusiastic support of minimum-wage increases when , according to the Bureau of Labor Statistics , the average union worker makes about $22.00 per hour, and there are few , if any , union members making minimum wage? There are several reasons. First, many union contracts are written so that an increase in minimum wage will trigger an increase in the union wage. One formula used sets baseline union wages as a percentage over the federal or state minimum wage. Another common formula uses a flat wage premium over the minimum wage. Other contracts stipulate that the employer and the union must re-negotiate wages in the event of a federal or state minimum-wage increase. Unions also benefit because minimum wage increases restrict competing businesses from hiring lower-skilled workers that may have only been cost-effective at a lower wage. Ultimately, this reduces competition from workers who might contend for union jobs. In short, an increase in the minimum wage equals an increase in union wages, which in turn equals increased revenue to the unions in the form of union dues. And where does much of that union revenue go? According to the Center for Responsive Politics, a total of $158 million went to the Democrat party in the last election alone. That's about all you need to know.

Conclusion

Nobel Prize-winning economist Milton Friedman said, "One of the great mistakes is to judge policies and programs by their intentions rather than their results." On the surface, minimum-wage laws seem like a natural way to help the working poor and reduce poverty. Unfortunately, empirical evidence indicates that minimum-wage increases are not effective at alleviating poverty, and usually result in more harm to the people they are purported to help. All it will accomplish is higher consumer prices, reduced business profits, and reduced employment levels. Those that stand to lose the most, as stated earlier, are lower-skilled workers, the disabled, youth, and ethnic minorities.

Millions of people have lost their jobs because of minimum-wage increases. The only apparent successes attributable to prior minimum-wage increases are those of the unions and the Democrats, who have successfully parlayed this issue into higher union revenues, increased negotiating power, and ultimately, higher campaign contributions.

The average American voter has little, if any, knowledge on this subject. Those who understand the overall impact are overwhelmingly against a minimum-wage increase. A recent poll, taken of voters who were apprised of the potential job losses, showed that sixty-eight percent of Republicans, fifty-three percent of independents, and fifty percent of Democrats oppose a minimum-wage increase if jobs are compromised. In order for voters of all parties to make an informed decision, this information needs to become common knowledge.

The only sure way to increase wages, without harming a significant portion of the workforce, is through job creation and economic growth. One needs to look no further than North Dakota to see the effect of job creation. Current entry-level jobs in North Dakota pay upwards of $17.00 per hour, and anyone who wants a job can find one. Rather than deflecting from the current dismal economic situation, Congress and the president need to take a more pro-active role in getting America back to work. A number of steps can be taken to increase wages and create jobs. Tax reforms, reduction in the immigration of unskilled workers, and the repeal of burdensome regulations, would likely result in a lower-wage tier that would—because of a demand for workers—double our current minimum wage.

CHAPTER SEVEN

Unemployment

One of the issues that concerns me the most, is the reporting of unemployment figures.

On the surface, reporting those figures seems straightforward. Each month, the U.S. Bureau of Labor Statistics (BLS) releases a report detailing everything we could ever want to know about the employment situation. The media dutifully relays that information to the American public. How could anything be easier than that? It is what it is, right? Well, no. The unemployment rate being reported by the mainstream media is not representative of the overall employment picture. The data they report does not expose the entire employment situation, and the data collection methodology is suspect. Once you read this chapter, you will never look at the reported unemployment number the same again.

Most people are not likely to research something as mundane as unemployment reports. I was one of them. However, I kept hearing about falling unemployment rates, and a growing economy with millions of new jobs. The problem is, I just wasn't seeing the evidence this was true. Everything I saw indicated the economy was getting worse. I had heard some radio talk-show hosts discuss unemployment discrepancies in the past, but had never taken the time to do my own research. I decided to investigate. This is a brief outline of what I found. I will start with the basics.

National unemployment surveys began in 1940. At that time, it was known as the Monthly Report of Unemployment. It was later renamed Current Population Survey (CPS) and is still the source of the unemployment data used by the Bureau of Labor Statistics (BLS) for their reports today. The data provided by the CPS is obtained via telephone surveys of 60,000 households, which represents about 110,000 individuals, in approximately 800 geographic areas nationwide. Every month, one-fourth of the households in the sample are changed, so that no household is interviewed for more than four consecutive months. After a household is interviewed for four consecutive months, that household isn't interviewed again for eight months. Then that household is interviewed for the same four calendar months a year later, before leaving the study for good.

Think about that. With all of our current technology and sophisticated reporting capabilities . . . we are still using the same data collection method we used in 1940. It seems unlikely that the BLS could arrive at accurate numbers by surveying *less than one-tenth of one percent* of the labor force. But that's how it's done. The BLS claims that "the chances are 90 out of 100 that the monthly estimate of unemployment from the sample is within about 300,000 of the figure obtainable from a total census." Well, that makes me feel much better. I have not been able to verify whether or not they are still calling on rotary-dial phones.

Once the data is compiled, the BLS releases the report on a monthly basis, which provides all relevant employment information for the prior five months, as well as a comparative month from the previous year. The report is presented with and without seasonal adjustments, and is broken out by race, sex, and age in each category. There are a number of categories, some of which portray the true jobs' situation better than others. The following, which I will explain in detail, are the categories that present the most accurate picture of the unemployment situation:

- The U-6 unemployment rate (The media reports the U-3 number)

- The labor-force participation rate

- The number of people not in the labor force

- Those working part-time for economic and non-economic reasons

Unemployment Rate

In 1976, the Bureau of Labor Statistics developed a set of seven reporting categories with regard to the unemployment data, allowing the entire labor force to be represented.

The BLS later revised the categories, which reduced the number from seven to six, but added the requirement that "discouraged workers" must have sought work within the prior year in order to be counted as "unemployed." These are the six unemployment categories and their definitions:

- **U-1**, persons unemployed fifteen weeks or longer, as a percentage of the civilian labor force

- **U-2**, job losers and persons who finished working at temporary jobs, as a percentage of the civilian labor force

- **U-3**, total unemployed, as a percentage of the civilian labor force (this is the category used for the official unemployment rate)

- **U-4**, total unemployed plus discouraged workers, as a percentage of the civilian labor force

- **U-5**, total unemployed, plus discouraged workers, plus all other marginally attached workers, as a percentage of the civilian labor force

- **U-6**, total unemployed, plus all marginally attached workers, plus discouraged workers, plus total employed part time for economic reasons, as a percentage of the civilian labor force

The unemployment number reported by the mainstream media is virtually always the U-3 number. This is not an accurate reflection of unemployment because it omits millions of discouraged workers, marginally attached workers, and those employed part-time for economic reasons, all of which are "unemployed" or "underemployed" people. The U-6 number provides the most accurate accounting of the unemployment picture, because these people are included:

Discouraged workers

These are individuals not currently looking for work because they believe no jobs are available for them.

Marginally attached to the labor force

These people were not in the labor force, but wanted work and were available for work, and had looked for a job in the prior twelve months. They are not counted as unemployed because they had not looked for work in the last four weeks preceding the survey.

Part-time for economic reasons

These are individuals who were working part-time because their hours had been cut or because they were unable to find a full-time job.

When these people are counted, the unemployment rate increases dramatically. In September 2014, the U-3 unemployment rate that was reported was 5.9 percent. The U-6 number for that same period was 11.8 percent.

Labor Force Participation Rate

Aside from the U-6 unemployment number, there are several other numbers in the BLS reports that are equally as important as economic indicators. The first is the labor-force participation rate, which is defined by the BLS as the percentage of working age adults (16 and older) who are employed part-time or full-time. As more people stop looking for work, this number will drop.

At the same time the mainstream media was reporting positive job creation trends in 2014, the labor force participation rate was at its lowest level in more than thirty-six years. It has dropped from 65.5 percent to 62.7 percent since Obama took office. That is not a good statistic if you want to brag about job creation.

Not In The Labor Force

Those considered to be "not in the labor force" include people who have quit looking for work, discouraged workers, those who have not looked for work in the four-week period preceding the survey, and those unable to look for work due to personal reasons. Once again, these people are not counted among the unemployed.

As of September 2014, there were 92,584,000 people not in the workforce, an all-time record. That number represents an increase of more than eleven million since January 2009.

Part-Time For Economic Reasons

This category refers to those who worked one to thirty-four hours during the reference week for an economic reason such as slack work or unfavorable business conditions, the inability to find full-time work, or seasonal declines in demand. This category will be of particular interest as the mandates of the Affordable Care Act are rolled out. Many employers are likely to cut full-time jobs, opting for part-time and contract workers, in order to avoid the excessive costs and penalties associated with Obamacare. Those who work part-time for non-economic reasons are also likely to increase, depending upon how their jobs are classified.

Unemployment Under Obama

The mainstream media is quick to point out that the unemployment rate is dropping, and millions of jobs are being created. I wish that were true. Unfortunately, as the saying goes, "You can put lipstick on a pig, but it's still a pig."

Aside from presiding over the worst economic recovery in history, Obama's employment numbers are just plain bad.

President Obama states that he has created eight million new jobs, which would be somewhat true if he had taken office in February 2010. But, as I recall, he took office in January 2009, which means he is responsible for the nearly four million jobs lost during his first thirteen months in office. His actual job creation as of July 2014 is just over 4.2 million, of which, most have been entry-level or part-time jobs. During that same period, more than eleven million people left the labor force. Obama's labor-force participation rate is the worst since Jimmy Carter was president.

No one has fared well under this administration. The labor-force participation rate for whites has dropped from 65.9 percent to 62.8 percent, with more than seven million whites leaving the work force. White teen unemployment is virtually unchanged at 18.7 percent.

The black labor-force participation rate is down from 63.4 percent to 61.7 percent. More than one-and-a-half million Blacks have left the work force. Black female unemployment is actually much worse since Obama took office, jumping from 9.2 percent 10.6

percent as of August 2014, despite the number leaving the workforce. At the same time, black teenage unemployment was 32.8 percent. Overall, the black unemployment rate is more than double that of whites, and the gap has actually widened during Obama's tenure.

Among Hispanics, the labor-force participation rate has dropped from 67.5 percent to 65.9 percent. More than two-and-a-half million Hispanics have left the work force. Teen unemployment for Hispanics was twenty-four percent as of September 2014.

A Great Month?

When the June 2014 unemployment numbers were released, the mainstream media could not wait to share the good news. The unemployment rate had dropped to 6.1 percent and a survey of businesses showed 288,000 new jobs. The celebration was on. For all the American public knew, this was great economic news. But was it? The answer is a resounding "no."

According to the Bureau of Labor Statistics, the labor-force participation rate for June 2014 was 62.8 percent, the lowest in thirty-six years. It hasn't been below that since the Carter presidency.

When Barack Obama took office, the labor-force participation rate was 65.5 percent. If that rate had remained constant, the June U-3 unemployment rate would have been 10.3 percent, and the U-6 rate would have reached nearly twenty percent.

The total number of Americans sixteen and older, who did not have a job in the last four weeks, was 92,120,000, up from 81,023,000 when Obama took office. This is a record for the most people not in the labor force. None of these people were counted as unemployed.

Also in June, the number of people taking part-time jobs, because they couldn't find full-time jobs, increased by 275,000. So, out of the 288,000 jobs created in June, 275,000 were part-time.

It gets worse. A total of 523,000 full-time jobs were lost in June 2014. At the same time, the number of people working part-time for non-economic reasons rose by 840,000, which is the largest increase since 1993. It will likely continue to increase as more of the Affordable Care Act mandates are implemented.

Virtually all of the reduction in the U-3 unemployment rate since 2009 is the result of the drop in the labor-force participation rate. There is no significant net job creation. The number is going down because so many people have quit looking for work and are no longer counted. The actual U-6 unemployment rate for June was 12.1 percent, a far cry from the 6.1 percent the media reported. Even at the questionable 6.1 percent figure, Obama is still well-behind George W. Bush, whose average unemployment rate during his eight years in office was 5.3 percent. In his first five years, Obama averaged 8.6 percent.

Teens and Unemployment

As I was doing the research for this chapter, I came across some facts about the effects of minimum-wage increases on teens. Although I have a complete chapter devoted to minimum wage, I wanted to approach the subject from a different angle in this chapter.

A study done in 2006 found that employment for teens in small businesses fell by an estimated 4.6 to 9.0 percent for every ten-percent increase in minimum wage. A similar study conducted in 2007, estimated employment would be reduced by as much as 6.6 percent for black and Hispanic teens, for every ten-percent minimum-wage increase.

Using U.S. Census Bureau data from May 2013 to April 2014, the Employment Policy Institute found excessively high unemployment rates in several major U.S. cities among teens without a high school diploma. Although it may not be a primary cause, most of the cities cited in the study had a minimum wage higher than the federal minimum wage.

The average unemployment rate for all workers, both skilled and unskilled, without a high-school diploma, was about eleven percent during the study period. All teens, sixteen to nineteen-years-old, averaged a 21.78 percent unemployment rate. Given those numbers, it would appear the most toxic combination is being young, unskilled, and in a higher-wage market that demands its money's worth.

In the Portland, Oregon area, where the minimum wage is above $9.00 an hour, the unemployment rate for sixteen- to nineteen-year-olds without a high-school diploma was 53.8 percent.

In the Riverside, California area, where the minimum wage was $8.00 per hour at the time of the study, the unemployment rate for sixteen- to nineteen-year-olds without a high-school diploma was 54.2 percent. As of July 1, 2014, California's minimum wage was increased to $9.00 per hour. If history is an indicator, don't be surprised if the unemployment rate for this group goes up.

Using the current proposed minimum wage increase from $7.25 to $10.10 per hour, let me give you an example of what happens to young unskilled workers when minimum wages are increased:

Bob Smith owns a fast food restaurant. He has twenty employees, who have varying skill levels. He has ten unskilled workers making $7.25 per hour, and ten more advanced workers who make $10.00 per hour. Every employee works thirty hours per week. Bob's total payroll is $5,175.00 per week. In order for Bob to pay his bills and make a living, he needs to realize a gross profit of $50,000.00 per month, which he is currently doing, with no room to spare. Now, he is told the minimum wage must be increased to $10.10 per hour. Since he has no room in his budget, he has three choices: 1) raise his prices, 2) reduce employee hours 3) reduce the number of employees. If he is in a business where increasing prices will lose business, he is forced to cut hours or employees. Since the more skilled employees can produce $10.10 per hour worth of goods or services, he simply gives them a ten-cent raise. That leaves him enough room in his budget for seven of the remaining ten employees. Bob fires his three least productive employees, all of which are unskilled teenagers. He may fire more, if the remaining workers are unable to justify the new wage. At that point he simply gives the remaining employees additional hours. The result is always the same: the lowest-skilled employees are the first to go, which in most cases means the teenagers.

Liberals will argue he should "do the right thing" and just increase prices and keep everyone working. Unfortunately, when you increase prices, you lose business. When you lose business, you lose income. When you lose income, you become further indebted. The more indebted you become, the more likely you are to go out of business. Then everyone loses their jobs. Sorry Liberals, but that's how the world works . . . unless you are General Motors.

Conclusion

When it comes to unemployment, it's obvious that what we are being told by the balance of the media does not match our personal observations. We are presented with tales of massive job creation and a rapidly growing economy. In reality, there are few jobs being created. Those which are created are entry-level and part-time. Millions of people have left the workforce, unable to find any reasonable job. Millions of others, with college educations, can't find work in their chosen fields. A college diploma no longer guarantees you a good job, or any job. You can't get a job that's not there, and you didn't rack up that student-loan debt so that you could work part-time. If the job market is as rosy as the media tells us, why are so many people with college degrees forced to accept menial jobs that don't even cover their obligations?

A recent Pew Research Poll found that thirty-six percent of millennials, aged 18-31, were still living with their parents—the highest number in almost fifty years.

It speaks volumes when you hear Nancy Pelosi say, "Unemployment benefits creates jobs faster than almost any other initiative you can name." Or when Barack Obama is quoted as saying, " However many jobs might be generated by a Keystone pipeline, they're going to be a lot fewer than the jobs that are created by extending the payroll tax cut and extending unemployment insurance." These are people who apparently don't understand economics. They also chose to surround themselves with people who have no private-sector work experience. Ninety percent of this administration has not worked in the private sector. This is what you get.

They don't understand that high corporate tax rates and a mountain of burdensome regulations will stifle business development and job growth. Maybe they haven't heard that corporations are expecting the mandates within the Affordable Care Act to add an estimated $4800 to $5900 per employee to their cost of doing business. I guess they don't understand why the only jobs being created are part-time jobs. Apparently, they also don't understand that minimum-wage increases are job killers, and that the only way to effectively increase wages is through job creation in a free market. They would only have to look as far as North Dakota, for an example. Perhaps they do understand, and simply choose to ignore the facts, while creating an ever-expanding base of government dependency.

Regardless of who is president, or which party is in power, the rules shouldn't change. The true employment situation needs to be judged using the criteria laid out in this chapter. Job creation does not include a mass exodus from the workforce. It also does not mean you only create entry-level and part-time jobs. Job creation is one area where Republicans can excel, but we too, must be held accountable.

CHAPTER EIGHT

Income Inequality

I continue to be amazed at the ability of the Left to create serious social issues where there are none. Income inequality is a prime example. Liberals have continued to use emotional rhetoric for years to create envy, resentment, and a perceived unfairness between the "have" and the "have not" sectors of our society. All this, in an effort to secure the latter as part of their voting base. Rather than being pro-active and creating an atmosphere where the poor can be involved in improving their own situation, they've spent decades and trillions of dollars trying to "fix" the problem by creating a dependency on government. Nowhere else does the entitlement mentality expose itself with such vigor.

As I stated earlier, the purpose of this book is to educate. This chapter will lead you to three conclusions: 1) some income inequality is necessary; 2) the actual income gap has been vastly exaggerated, and; 3) Democratic policies have done more to widen the gap than reduce it.

In a speech given on December 4, 2013, President Obama stated, "A dangerous and growing inequality and lack of upward mobility" is "the defining challenge of our time." That statement speaks volumes about the reasons for America's economic woes. Instead of naming economic growth and job creation as the defining challenge of our time, he concentrates on a virtual non-issue like income inequality.

Income inequality is a fact of life. Most Americans understand that income disparity is healthy in a free-market society. Those who produce more, by virtue of their own ideas and actions, earn the wealth they create and deserve to keep it.

Literal income equality is impossible. Most families don't even have income equality among themselves. Any potential "fix" for income inequality would result in the collapse of the entire economic structure of our country. You can't make, or keep, everyone wealthy. The only way to make everyone equal is to make sure everyone is poor. Socialism has never worked. No one has ever benefited from making a rich person poor. People are not created equal. We all make choices throughout our lives that determine the outcome of our future financial situation. Differences in one's physical capability, work ethic, intellectual level, drive, and ambition, are all factors that will determine a person's future prosperity. As we get older, other factors come into play: education, skill level, career choice, family situations, and other interests that will affect our earnings. Everyone is different and we should not expect the same results from each and every person. If a person chooses to work part-time in order to spend more time with family, they should not expect to earn as much as the person who works full-time. They both get their respective "rewards", however they will not, or should not, be equal in the monetary sense.

Likewise, those who further their education, or develop new skills, should not be penalized by having their money "redistributed" to those with less ambition.

The president should focus on "income mobility" rather than income inequality. Income mobility is the ability to move from one income quintile (The Census Bureau divides income demographics into fifths, called quintiles) to another throughout the course of one's life. People in the bottom quintile tend to be those who are entering the job market in the early stages of their career, generally teenagers, unskilled immigrants, or people without a high-school diploma. This quintile also includes part-time workers. As the people in the bottom quintile become more skilled and more productive, they tend to move into the higher income quintiles. From 1999 to 2007, approximately sixty percent of those in the bottom quintile moved up to a higher quintile. Conversely, in the last four decades, about forty percent of those in the top quintile have dropped to lower quintiles. There is even more movement as you get closer to the top. Of the top 400 income earners in the United States during the last forty years, only fifteen percent were able to stay in the top 400 for longer than two years. The media would like us to think that the rich stay rich and the poor stay poor, which is obviously not the case.

Although it is true that the top quintile has seen a faster rise in income in recent years, the growth rates for income have increased in every quintile. If you use all income and tax liability figures, and account for the demographic disparities in the Census Bureau numbers, income inequality actually declined sixty-eight percent between 1983 and 2009.

Since 1970, the GDP (Gross Domestic Product) of the United States increased over 300 percent, which means that everyone, regardless of income category, has benefited because the "size of the pie" has continued to grow.

A CBO (Congressional Budget Office) report, released in October 2011, showed that family income, including benefits, on average, experienced a sixty-two percent gain above inflation from 1979 to 2007. All five quintiles experienced gains. The average median household income grew by thirty-five percent during that period. Since 1970, the purchasing power of the dollar for the bottom quintile increased almost eleven percent, and the quality of the purchases have improved significantly, which you will see later in this chapter.

The most important factor is that all income categories grew, and they grew during a period of rapid globalization, which is even more remarkable.

The Problem with Census Bureau Figures

The most common research source used by media outlets, with regard to income inequality, is the U.S. Census Bureau reports. The Census Bureau ranks household income from highest to lowest, and divides the population into five groups mentioned earlier, called quintiles, and determines the share of total income received in each quintile. These numbers appear to be straight-forward, however, the census data is marred by four problems that lead to a substantial overstatement of income inequality. The problems are as follows:

1. Conventional census income figures are incomplete and omit many types of cash and non-cash income.

2. Conventional census figures do not factor in the equalizing effects of taxation.

3. Census Bureau quintiles do not contain equal numbers of persons, which greatly magnifies the apparent level of income inequality.

4. The Census Bureau numbers fail to recognize the huge disparity in the number of hours worked in each quintile.

Any one of these four issues would have a significant impact on income disparity calculations. Combined, they completely distort the true income-inequality picture.

First of all, the Census Bureau figures use what they call "money income", which does not include several types of income. Money income omits public assistance, such as food stamps, public housing, school-lunch programs, and any earned-income-tax credits. It also omits a portion of capital gains income.

Second, money income is based on pre-tax dollars. Federal and state taxes, property taxes, and social security taxes all have a greater impact on the top quintile than the bottom quintile, which pays little, if any.

Another problem is that Census Bureau quintiles are unequal in size, because they are based on a count of *households* rather than persons. Media reports based on Census Bureau figures fail to factor in that American households in the top quintile have, on average, almost five times more working family members than the bottom quintile. These people are also far more likely to be well-educated, married, and working more hours. Low-income households tend to be single persons with little or no wage income.

The top quintile has sixty-five percent more persons than the bottom quintile. Instead of each quintile representing equal fifths of our society, the top quintile is actually representing over twenty-four percent, while the bottom quintile represents less than fifteen percent. Obviously, the huge demographic variance will have a significant impact on the income disparity between the two quintiles.

Finally, the Census Bureau figures fail to account for the difference in the number of hours of work performed in each quintile. Most media reports assume that working-age adults in each quintile perform the same average number of paid work hours. In reality, the annual number of hours of employed labor in the top quintile is about double that of the lowest quintile. Even without factoring in the generally higher wages, the sheer volume of work hours in the top quintile, by itself, would equate to a significant income gap between the two quintiles.

Using conventional Census Bureau figures, the top quintile is shown as receiving about $14.00 in income for every $1.00 in the bottom quintile. However, once all incomes are counted, and taxes are considered, the ratio drops to about $8.00 for every $1.00 of income. If you then adjust the quintiles to contain equal numbers of persons, the ratio of incomes between the top and bottom quintiles drops to just over $4.00 to $1.00—a large portion of which is due to the disparity in total work hours. If the adults in both quintiles worked the same number of hours, the final income disparity gap would fall to just over $3.00 for the top quintile, compared to $1.00 for the bottom quintile, which just about wipes out the inequality narrative.

The Obama Effect

Few things influence our poverty level, and ultimately the condition of the bottom income quintile, as much as job creation. Only three percent of Americans who have a full-time job live in poverty. As such, the Obama administration has made a significant contribution to widening the income gap. There are currently more than ninety-two million people who are not in the workforce, an increase of more than eleven million since Obama took office. Of the six million jobs created during Obama's "recovery", the vast majority have been low-wage and part-time jobs. The percentage of part-time workers is up forty-three percent. The number of people on food stamps has increased by almost fifty percent. And during his first five years in office, the average payroll for American workers, measured in inflation-adjusted dollars, only increased 0.3 percent. All of these factors have contributed to a reduction in income for the bottom quintile.

Conversely, corporate profits and the incomes of their principles and employees have increased dramatically. While the rest of the country has struggled, Wall Street has enjoyed robust growth, courtesy of the "stimulus" plan, round after round of quantitative easing, and artificially low interest rates. The financial industry as a whole has done very well, as has the stock market. Capital investment income has increased significantly faster than wage income as a percentage. Most of the players in this arena are in the top income quintile. So basically, under Obama, the rich got richer.

The official measure of income inequality is the Census Bureau's Gini Index, also known as the Gini coefficient. The Gini coefficient measures equality in income distribution on a scale of zero to one. A rating of zero would indicate perfect equality in income disbursement, and a rating of one would indicate total inequality, with all income in the U.S. going to a single household.

Of the last three presidents, Bill Clinton had the highest Gini average (52.48) during his two terms in office. The Gini average improved to 51.64 during George W. Bush's presidency, then rose to an average of 52.05 during Barack Obama's first term. Given its importance as the official measurement of income inequality, you would think the media would reference it more frequently. However, the media's narrative gains nothing as a result, so this index is usually avoided.

How Poor is Poor?

Apparently, I'm pretty naïve when it comes to understanding the condition of America's poor. When the Left talks about the poor, it takes me back to my first couple of years out of college. I was living in Salem, Oregon and working for a bank. I was taking home less than $500.00 per month. I shared a small rental home in an alley with another young guy who made even less than I did. We had a stereo and a refrigerator, but no T.V., no dishwasher, and no microwave. After rent, utilities, and my car payment, I had little discretionary income left over. If it hadn't been for the kindness of my girlfriend's parents, and the Vietnamese refugees across the alley, my entire diet would have consisted of chili and Campbell's Soup.

That was my experience, and that's how I envisioned the plight of today's poor. You know . . . rice and beans and government cheese. That's the impression the media gives.

Then, as I was doing research for this book, I stumbled upon a report released in September 2011 titled "Understanding Poverty in the United States: Surprising Facts About America's Poor." This report gleaned information from a number of government reports with regard to the conditions of Americans living in "poverty." What they found was startling.

Based on the media portrayal, most Americans view "poverty" as destitution . . . an inability to provide adequate clothing, food and shelter for their family. However, of the forty-six-million people classified as impoverished by the Census Bureau, only a small percentage would be considered destitute. While real material hardship does occur, the scope and severity of the problem has been greatly exaggerated by the media and the Left. Here are some facts that were uncovered in this report:

- 99.6 percent of poor households have a refrigerator

- 98 percent have a stove or oven

- 98 percent have a TV

- 92.3 percent of poor households have a microwave

- 81.6 percent of poor households have an air conditioner

- 74.1 percent own a car or truck; 30.6% own more than one

- 70.6 percent own a VCR

- 64.5 percent own a DVD player

- 50.2 percent own a personal computer; 15.9% own more than one

- 53.9 percent own a video game system (XBox, PS2, etc.)

- 42.6 percent have internet service

- 63.7 percent have cable or satellite TV

- 39.7 percent have a dishwasher

- 33.7 percent have a big screen plasma or LCD TV

- 34.3 percent own a non-portable stereo system

- 23.1 percent have a DVR system, such as TIVO

Other findings were equally surprising. America's poor, on average, live in housing that totals 515 square-feet per person, which is about forty percent more per person than that of the average European household not in poverty. Forty-two percent of poor households in the U.S. own their own home.

The data also finds there is little or no evidence of poverty-induced malnutrition in the United States. Among poor children, the average nutrient consumption closely resembles that of the upper middle class.

My purpose is not to make light of poor people. Lord knows I've been there. But, if we are going to properly address the issue of poverty in America, it needs to be done honestly and accurately. Problems can't be solved if we don't know the full extent of the problem. Gross exaggeration of the extent and severity of poverty will not benefit anyone, including the poor. The public, as well as the policymakers, get the balance of their information from the media. Unfortunately, the media seldom reports all of the facts on this issue. If we are to create effective policies to help those in need, it needs to be done using all available data.

The Democrats War On The Poor

For as much effort as the Left puts into championing the cause of income inequality, they do a poor job in their own backyards. It should not be surprising that the cities with the highest levels of income inequality are all cities controlled by Democrats, all of which voted overwhelming to re-elect Obama in 2012. Here are the top ten cities for income inequality:

1. Atlanta   (71 percent voted for Obama)

2. San Francisco   (83.4 percent voted for Obama)

3. Miami   (61.5 percent voted for Obama)

4. Boston   (79 percent voted for Obama)

5. Washington D.C. (91 percent voted for Obama)

6. New York   (81 percent voted for Obama)

7. Oakland   (78.7 percent voted for Obama)

8. Chicago   (85 percent voted for Obama)

9. Los Angeles   (69.7 percent voted for Obama)

10. Baltimore   (87.4 percent voted for Obama)

Only three Republican cities were in the top fifty, the highest being Phoenix at number thirty-eight.

Conclusion

America has an entrepreneurial culture and the ability to produce more innovative products at a higher productivity level than any country in the world. As such, we have a number of people who have accumulated massive wealth as a result of their efforts. If that creates a huge income disparity between the top one percent and the rest of us, so be it. We shouldn't care. These are the people who are creating thousands of jobs, which in turn give thousands of employees the opportunity for upward mobility. These are the people who are turning the wheels of American prosperity.

For decades, Americans have been responsible for the highest levels of personal-income growth of any nation in the history of mankind. This happened because Americans have been free to invent and create, research and develop, start and grow industries, and create an ever-increasing demand for workers. We have done this without income redistribution, extreme environmentalism, or government overreach.

Today, more than ever, the government is determined to impose regulations that will ultimately bankrupt numerous companies, create additional unemployment, increase food and energy costs, and lower our overall standard of living.

Companies are finding it increasingly difficult to do business in the United States. In the last five years, we have seen mountains of new EPA regulations, ongoing Obamacare mandates, hundreds of new regulations from other entities like the Federal Trade Commission and the National Labor Relations Board, and the ongoing effects of the Dodd-Frank Bill. The new EPA regulations alone, since Obama took office, total 24,915 pages and approximately twenty-four million words. By comparison, the entire seven volumes of the Harry Potter book series have less than 1.1 million words. No politician can read and assimilate the information prior to its discussion. This level of regulatory burden is more than many companies choose to deal with.

Other liberal policies have led to a suppression of income at the lower end of the income scale. The influx of low-skilled, low-income immigrants over the past thirty years has disproportionately impacted the bottom income quintile.

Another problem is a substandard educational system in America. Improving our education system, especially in the inner cities, would do more to reduce income disparity than any other public policy fix. Allowing school choice and eliminating self-defeating programs like Common Core would have a positive impact on our children's futures.

The Democratic Party's solution to reducing income inequality involves a redistribution of income through increases in government assistance and higher taxes. This "solution" will discourage hiring and investment, and will depress economic growth and opportunity.

In contrast, if we focus on policies that improve economic opportunity, everyone will have the ability to benefit, especially those in the lower income households.

The true disparity between the highest and lowest income quintiles has been greatly exaggerated, and there is no reasonable evidence that a reduction in income inequality will ever increase the economic well-being for the majority of Americans.

Income mobility is far more important than income inequality, and based on studies of forty-million tax returns, done by economists at Harvard and U.C. Berkeley, income mobility has not changed in thirty years.

CHAPTER NINE

Abortion

The subject of abortion may be one of the most hotly debated subjects in all of politics. A significant number of votes are cast in every election, by people in both parties, based on their respective candidate's view on this single issue. Pro-abortion candidates contend that a fetus is not actually a human life and that a woman has the right to decide what happens with her body. Anti-abortion candidates believe life begins at conception, and as such, a fetus has the right to life. In recent years, the support for abortion has continued to dwindle as more information has become available with regard to the risks associated with abortion, and the details of the various procedures themselves, which I cover later in this chapter.

Thirty years ago, those who held a pro-life view were in the minority. However, a Gallup poll taken in May 2009 showed that, for the first time, a significantly greater percentage of Americans identified themselves as pro-life.

A Gallup poll released in May 2014, indicated that forty-seven percent of Americans considered themselves "pro-choice", and forty-six percent considered themselves "pro-life." Those are the numbers the media reported. However, that same poll revealed that fifty-nine percent felt that abortion should either always be illegal, or illegal except in the case of rape, incest, or when the life of the mother was in danger. They also supported overturning Roe v. Wade. So in reality, fifty-nine percent are actually "pro-life."

A *CNN* poll, taken two months earlier, also found that fifty-nine percent of Americans felt abortion should be illegal, or legal only in the case of rape, incest, or when the life of the mother is in danger.

A *CBS* poll, released in July 2013, shows that Americans overwhelmingly (sixty-one percent to thirty-seven percent) want more limits on abortions.

Millions of women in America have had an abortion. It is not our place to judge them. Many of us bought into the narrative that was being portrayed by the likes of Planned Parenthood. The abortion industry has been reluctant to provide women with any negative information related to abortion. Women with unintended pregnancies, and those who advocate "choice", have not been given the facts. As a result, many women have blindly elected to have the procedure, only to suffer long-term physical and emotional trauma. Both pre-abortive and post-abortive women are often misled by clinic counselors, and never properly informed of the potential dangers, such as an increased risk of future breast cancer. This lack of honesty on the part of the abortion industry may indicate they have less regard for women's health than they do for money and politics. The purpose of this chapter is to educate. When people understand the risks associated with abortion, the reproductive science, and the brutality of the procedure itself, it often changes their position. Let's be honest. Abortion is a tool that allows sexual convenience at the cost of a human life.

I am totally for "choice" for women in most aspects of their lives, except for the ones that involve the well-being of another innocent person. If I thought there was only one body involved, I would likely be pro-choice. Arguments that are based on "privacy" or "choice" indicate a lack of knowledge on this issue. The entire abortion controversy can be boiled down to one simple question: at what point does a human become a human?

The Science

Abortion advocates have long argued that "no one knows when life begins" and that only a "blob of tissue" exists during the early stages of pregnancy. However, virtually all scientists agree—and science documents—the fact that life begins at conception.

At the moment when a human sperm penetrates a human egg, a new entity comes into existence. This first cell is called a zygote, and it is the earliest developmental stage of the human embryo. It is composed of human DNA and molecules, and thus human, not some other species. It also has its own unique genetic composition, different from any other human, including the mother.

Some abortion advocates will concede that life begins at conception, but still argue that the embryo in the womb is not a "human", which is a totally philosophical view that runs contrary to known science.

Human embryos develop at an incredibly rapid pace. The brain and heart begin forming only two weeks after conception, usually before the mother even realizes she is pregnant. At about twenty-two days after conception, that heart begins to circulate its own blood, different than that of the mother, and its heartbeat can be detected on ultrasound. At six weeks, the child's eyes, nose, mouth, and tongue have formed. Brain activity can be detected at six to seven weeks. By the end of the eighth week, the child has developed all of its organs and bodily structures. By the tenth week, the child can make bodily movements. There is literally no part of this process that is not human.

Roe V. Wade

As most people know, abortion under most circumstances became legal in the United States with the 1973 Supreme Court ruling in the landmark case of Roe v. Wade. The suit was filed in Texas on behalf of the plaintiff, Norma McCorvey (alias: Jane Roe) against the defendant, Henry Wade, the Dallas County District Attorney. The case was heard along with a companion case, Doe v. Bolton. Although they admitted that abortion is not in the text of the Constitution, the court ruled in a 7-2 decision that a right to privacy under the due process clause of the 14th Amendment extended to a woman's decision to have an abortion, as long as the woman's health was protected and the abortion performed before the fetus became "viable" (twenty-four weeks). They also ruled that the word "person" in the Constitution did not include a fetus.

Most people don't understand the full extent of Roe v. Wade. It granted a virtually unlimited right to abortion under which *any* abortion can be justified. The court ruled that abortion must be permitted for *any reason* a woman chooses until viability. After viability is reached, an abortion must still be permitted if an abortion doctor deems the abortion necessary to protect a woman's "health." The definition of "health" was defined in Doe v. Bolton as "all factors physical, emotional, psychological, familial, and the woman's age, relevant to the well-being of the patient." In other words, the court created the right to abort a child at any time, even past the point of viability, for "emotional" reasons. This ruling basically granted absolute power to the abortion doctors.

What most people don't know is that neither plaintiff took an active role in their respective cases. Sandra Cano (alias: Mary Doe) continues to assert that she was tricked into filing her suit, Doe v. Bolton, by over-zealous attorneys who were intent on getting abortion legalized. Once she realized what had transpired, she immediately set out to clear her name. She was actually a pro-life Christian at the time.

Norma McCorvey (Jane Roe) never had an abortion, but soon went on to work at an abortion clinic in Texas. While working at the clinic, she befriended a minister who worked at an Operation Rescue (anti-abortion) facility that had moved in next door to the abortion clinic.

One day, while visiting the minister at the Operation Rescue building, she saw a poster showing images of human fetuses at various stages of development. These are her words:

> I was sitting in O.R.'s offices when I noticed a fetal development poster. The progression was so obvious, the eyes were so sweet. It hurt my heart, just looking at them. I ran outside and finally, it dawned on me. "Norma,",I said to myself, "they're right." I had worked with pregnant women for years. I had been through three pregnancies and deliveries myself. I should have known. Yet something in that poster made me lose my breath. I kept seeing the picture of that tiny, 10-week-old embryo, and I said to myself, "that's a baby!" It's as if blinders just fell off my eyes and I suddenly understood the truth—that's a baby! I felt crushed under the truth of this realization. I had to face up to the awful reality. Abortion wasn't about "products of conception." It wasn't about "missed periods." It was about children being killed in their mother's wombs. All those years I was wrong. Signing that affidavit, I was wrong. Working in an abortion clinic, I was wrong. No more of the first trimester, second trimester stuff. Abortion—at any point—was wrong. It was so clear. Painfully clear."

Norma immediately quit her job at the abortion clinic and became a pro-life advocate. Let that soak in for a minute. The plaintiff in Roe v. Wade, the most famous abortion case in history, never had an abortion, and is now a pro-life advocate. That's a mindset change of epic proportion, which seems to happen quite frequently when ill-informed people are presented with the facts.

In the five years following Roe v. Wade, the abortion rate in the U.S. rose by more than fifty percent.

Currently, a majority of Americans support overturning Roe v. Wade, which would not make abortion illegal, but would simply put the issue of abortion in the hands of the individual state's representatives, which are more likely to represent the will of the people.

One final part of Roe v. Wade that needs to be re-evaluated is the fact that the ruling was based on the premise that the states no longer needed to regulate abortion because the advances of modern medicine had made abortion relatively safe. The justices therefore concluded it would be unconstitutional to prevent physicians from providing abortions as a "health service" to women. Let's take a look at what we now know about the safety level of abortions.

Abortion Risks

Women considering an abortion need to know about the risks, both physically and psychologically. I believe that once women have gained a greater understanding of the medical risks associated with abortion, there will likely be a significant reduction in the number of abortions performed.

Despite numerous findings to the contrary, the abortion industry has continued to deny and censor any studies that indicate a correlation between abortion and breast cancer risk. What they do report are individual studies, usually done by pro-abortion researchers and institutions, showing no link between abortion and breast cancer, although they do state that "research is continuing."

Two of the most cited sources used by the media for information on abortion are Planned Parenthood and the Guttmacher Institute.

On its website, Planned Parenthood, the largest abortion provider in America, makes the following statement: "There are many myths about the risks of abortion. Here are the facts. Abortion does not cause breast cancer. Safe, uncomplicated abortion does not cause problems for future pregnancies such as birth defects, premature birth, or low birth weight babies, ectopic pregnancy, miscarriage, or infant death." Likewise, the website for the Guttmacher Institute, a slick and well-formatted site, made a similar claim. On a page titled "Facts on induced abortion in the United States", it listed numerous "facts" about abortion. As I was reading down the list of "facts", a couple of statements caught my attention. The first stated that various U.S. and British government panels have concluded there is no association between abortion and breast cancer. The other statement said "In repeated studies since the early 1980s, leading experts have concluded abortion does not pose a hazard to women's mental health." What? I couldn't believe what I was reading. What "experts" were these people talking to? I knew both of those statements were not true.

Since Planned Parenthood is the largest abortion provider in America, I assumed they would not willfully disclose any abortion risk, but why did the Guttmacher Institute make the same misleading statements?

At that point, I decided to research the Guttmacher Institute itself and the sources of the aforementioned "facts." As it turns out, the Guttmacher Institute is a research and propaganda arm of Planned Parenthood. Its namesake, Alan Guttmacher, was a former president of Planned Parenthood. The picture was starting to get clearer. Most of the "facts" listed on the website were actually written by Guttmacher Institute staff members. Some of the data was more than twenty years old.

The National Abortion Federation, the National Cancer Institute, the American Cancer Society, and Susan G. Komen for the cure, also claim that research clearly shows no link between abortion and the risk of breast cancer. As supporting "evidence", they all point to the findings of a 2003 workshop conducted by the National Cancer Institute.

What they have failed to disclose is that in 2009, the chief organizer of the above mentioned workshop, Dr. Louise Brinton, co-authored a research paper which included the following findings:

> In analyses of the 897 breast cancer cases (subtypes combined), the multivariate-adjusted odds ratios for examined risk factors were consistent with the effects observed in previous studies on younger women. Specifically, older age, family history of breast cancer, earlier menarche age, induced abortion, and oral contraceptive use were associated with an increased risk for breast cancer.

Only a handful of media outlets reported the findings. A story in Canada's *The Globe and Mail* stated the following:

> . . . a study released last fall by the respected Fred Hutchinson Cancer Research Institute in Seattle by a number of distinguished cancer experts including Louise Brinton, the Chief of the Hormonal and Reproductive Epidemiology Branch of the National Cancer Institute lists induced abortion as being "associated with an increased risk for breast cancer." Background documents further suggest that it increases the risk of the disease by 40 percent.

The fact is, there have been dozens of studies done that have found a cancer link. In 1996, Joel Brind, a professor of Biology and Endocrinology at Baruch College, released a report that combined the results of twenty-three separate studies that indicated at least a thirty-percent higher risk of breast cancer for women having had an abortion.

Another report, released in 2013, included thirty-six studies from fourteen provinces in China. Annual abortions in China exceed eight million, with 400 abortions for every 1000 live births. The report showed the risk of breast cancer increased by forty-four percent with one abortion, seventy-six percent with two abortions, and eighty-nine percent with three abortions. This is the most extensive study to date and, unlike some of the studies done in the United States, the Chinese have no motivation to manipulate or censor their findings.

There have been over fifty-five million abortions performed in the United States since Roe v. Wade. If you take the overall risk of breast cancer among women to be approximately ten percent, and then increase that risk by the forty-four percent reported in the Chinese study, you end up with an additional 4.4% of the women who have had an abortion that will likely end up getting cancer. Counting only the fifty-three percent of the women who have had one abortion since Roe v. Wade (approximately forty-seven percent had multiple abortions according to the U.S. Census Bureau), we get a total of 29.15 million women. We can assume an additional 4.4 % of those women got cancer who otherwise would not have gotten it. That brings us to a total 1,282,600 who ended up getting cancer as a direct result of having an abortion. At a conservative mortality rate of fifteen percent, which is lower than the historic mortality rate, you arrive at a total of more than 192,000 additional breast cancer deaths since 1973 as a result of having had a single abortion, let alone multiple abortions. That's a far cry from the zero risk stated by Planned Parenthood.

In addition to an increased risk of breast cancer, there are a number of other risks that women face by having an abortion. Here are the most common issues: uterine damage; pelvic inflammatory disease; future ectopic pregnancies; increased rate of preterm birth in future pregnancies; infertility; placental abruption; infection; psychological and emotional trauma; and death.

There is significant data to support each of these risks. The following is a brief summary of these risks:

Uterine Damage

In his book, *Abortion Practice*, Dr. Warren Hern notes "it may be argued that each abortion, no matter how carefully performed, results in a contaminated uterine cavity." And, "in medical practice, there are few surgical procedures given so little attention and so underrated in its potential hazard as abortion." Approximately two percent of all first-trimester surgical abortions result in a perforated uterus. And according to an article published in *American Journal of Obstetrics and Gynecology*, "approximately 2% to 10% of medical abortion patients will require surgical intervention for control of bleeding, resolution of incomplete expulsion, or termination of a continuing pregnancy."

The most common form of uterine damage, as a result of an abortion procedure, is the likelihood of hemorrhaging or conditions that predispose to hemorrhaging. In severe cases, a perforated uterus can cause life-threatening internal bleeding. Even if the perforation has healed, the resulting scar tissue may be weak and "blow out" during a subsequent pregnancy. A perforation of the uterus that lacerates a uterine artery may also cause the woman to bleed to death.

Pelvic Inflammatory Disease

PID is a term used to describe the inflammation of the uterus, fallopian tubes, or ovaries, and this can cause scarring with adhesions to nearby tissues and organs. This can lead to infertility, chronic pelvic pain, ectopic pregnancy, and occasionally will cause inflammation and the formation of scar tissue on the external surface of the liver (Fitzhugh-Curtis Syndrome). Ectopic pregnancy is the leading cause of pregnancy-related deaths among adult females. The Center for Disease Control released a report showing a dramatic increase in ectopic pregnancies as a result of PID that closely paralleled the increase in abortions during the 1970-1989 period. It has continued that parallel.

Increased Rate of Pre-term Birth in Future Pregnancies

Pre-term birth is the leading cause of neonatal death in the United States. It accounts for literally hundreds of thousands of deaths. There are 135 studies from around the world that link PTB to prior abortions. The pre-term birth rate in the United States prior to Roe v. Wade was about six percent. The PTB rate is now almost thirteen percent. Studies have indicated that a single, prior abortion increases the likelihood of a woman having a pre-term birth by thirty-six percent. The PTB rate among African-American women is double the rate of other women, which coincides with a higher abortion rate in that part of our population.

Placental Abruption

Placental abruption is a condition where the placental lining has separated from the uterus after twenty weeks of gestation, but prior to birth. It occurs in approximately one percent of the births worldwide. It is the most common pathological cause of late-pregnancy bleeding. In extreme cases, it can cause severe life-threatening blood loss. Shock can also occur, which may affect other vital organs.

Infection

There are several types of infections associated with abortion. Two of the more common types are endometritis and pelvic inflammatory disease.

Endometritis is an infection in the inner uterine wall. If not promptly treated, it can require hospitalization and impair future fertility. Endometritis is a major cause of maternal mortality.

In addition to the risks mentioned earlier regarding PID, about one out of ten women cannot become pregnant after having PID only once. After having PID three or more times, as many as seven out of ten women become infertile.

Psychological and Emotional Trauma

Abortion advocates often assert that women who have had an abortion feel a sense of relief, without any serious emotional trauma. The fact is, most women, including those who felt relief initially, will begin to have negative psychological and emotional issues within a matter of weeks. In less than two months after abortion, fifty-five percent of women expressed guilt, forty-four percent complained of nervous disorders, and thirty-five percent had experienced sleep disturbances. Almost one-third regretted having the abortion and eleven percent had already been put on prescription psychotropic medicine. Many other issues will often continue to manifest themselves throughout their lives.

Women who have undergone post-abortion counseling have reported over 100 major reactions to abortion. Among the most frequently reported reactions are: severe depression, loss of self-esteem, grief, self-destructive behavior, sleep disorders, sexual dysfunction, difficulty forming relationships, anxiety attacks, increased tendency towards violence, alcohol or drug abuse, eating disorders, social regression, suicidal thoughts or tendencies, and difficulty bonding with later children.

Among the most concerning of these reactions is the increase in self-destructive behavior. In a survey of 100 women suffering from post-abortion trauma, eighty percent expressed feelings of self-hatred, and sixty percent reported suicidal ideation, with twenty-eight percent actually attempting suicide. In the same study, forty-nine percent reported drug abuse and thirty-nine percent began to use, or increased, their use of alcohol. Of these, fourteen percent described themselves as "addicted."

A separate Canadian study, covering a five-year period, found that twenty-five percent of the post-abortion women studied sought psychiatric help as compared to only three percent in the control group.

Death

Although it's not as prevalent as some of the other risks associated with abortion, the risk is there nonetheless. Abortion advocates argue that abortion is safer than giving birth and that more women die giving birth than die having an abortion. That statement is absolutely true. Once again, it all comes down to what you are not being told. While the physical act of giving birth does have a higher mortality rate for the mother, studies show that the rate of death from future "natural causes" is only about half that of those women who have had an abortion. And this does not include the mortality of women with breast cancer who may have developed that cancer as a direct result of an abortion. A study of maternal deaths during the abortion procedure from the period 1991-1999 indicated that thirty-four percent of the deaths during that period were the result of infection, and twenty-two percent were the result of hemorrhaging. The long-term risks of death include complications from ectopic pregnancies, placental abruption, and prior uterine/cervical damage. Women who have had an abortion face a fifty-eight percent greater risk of dying during a later pregnancy.

Abortion Procedures

The type of procedure used in elective abortions is determined primarily by the length of gestation. Medical abortions, which are becoming more common, are only available through the first nine weeks of gestation. In 2011, twenty-three percent of all non-hospital abortions in the U.S., approximately 239,400, were early medication abortions. More than half of known abortion providers offer abortion pills.

The following is a brief description of the procedures used within the respective trimesters.

The First Trimester

Methotrexate and Misoprostol (MTX): A medical abortion procedure used within the first seven weeks of pregnancy. This combination of medicine is not as commonly used in U.S. as in other countries.

Mifepristone and Misoprostol: Also known as RU-486, the abortion pill, or Mifeprex. This is the medical abortion procedure most commonly used in the U.S. It can be used up to the first seven to nine weeks of pregnancy. It works by prohibiting the synthesis and functionality of progesterone, a hormone that is necessary to sustain early pregnancy. When the function of progesterone is compromised, the uterus contracts, the endometrium becomes incompatible with the implanted embryo, and the cervix softens to allow expulsion.

Manual Vacuum Aspiration (MVA): A procedure that can be used as early as three to twelve weeks since the last period, but is rarely used after nine weeks gestation. In this procedure, a cannula is inserted into the uterus, and is connected to an aspirator by a length of tubing. The aspirator provides the necessary suction to empty the uterus, pulling the fetus to pieces in the process. The cannula is rotated side to side, from the back of the uterus to the front, until the flow of tissue through the cannula and hose ceases. Only a local anesthesia is used on the cervix, which many believe to be a less invasive procedure.

Suction Curettage: Also known as dilation and curettage (D&C). A surgical procedure that can be used to terminate pregnancy up to sixteen weeks from the last period, although in actual practice it is seldom used after twelve weeks gestation. Approximately seventy-six percent of the abortions in the U.S. use this procedure. In this procedure, the mother's cervix is dilated until it is large enough to allow a cannula to be inserted into her uterus. Most North American abortionists dilate the cervix mechanically using tapered dilators. The cannula is a hollow plastic tube that is connected to a vacuum-type pump, which can produce suction up to twenty-nine times stronger than a household vacuum cleaner. The abortionist runs the tip of the cannula along the surface of the uterus causing the baby to be dislodged and sucked into the tube—either whole or in pieces—along with amniotic fluid and placenta. Any remaining parts are scraped out of the uterus with a surgical instrument called a curette. Another pass is then made through the uterus with the suction machine to make sure none of the body parts have been left behind.

The Second Trimester

Dilation and Curettage (D&C): See suction curettage above.

Dilation and Evacuation (D&E): A surgical procedure used to terminate pregnancy after sixteen-weeks gestation. Approximately ninety-six percent of all second-trimester abortions in the U.S. use this procedure. In this procedure the cervix is dilated and a speculum is inserted to allow for increased access and maneuverability with the forceps, which are used for the dismemberment and removal of the fetus. The rest of the fetus is then removed piece by piece, except for the skull, which must be collapsed prior to removal.

Induction Abortion: This is a rarely used procedure where salt water, urea, or potassium chloride is injected into the amniotic sac; prostaglandins are inserted into the vagina and Pitocin is injected intravenously.

The Third Trimester

Other than cases where the mother's life is at risk, most states have banned third-trimester or late-term abortions. If a late-term abortion is allowed, one of the following procedures is generally used.

Induction Abortion: See above.

Dilation and Extraction (D&X): Also known as a partial-birth abortion. It is a variation of the Dilation and Evacuation (D&E) procedure whereby the aborted fetus is delivered intact instead of in pieces. In this method, the skull is often crushed to allow removal of brain matter with a vacuum aspirator to allow for the passage of the skull through the cervix.

In Their Own Words

"Colored people are human weeds and they are to be exterminated." Margaret Sanger, Founder of Planned Parenthood

"The most successful, educational appeal to the negro is through a religious appeal. We do not want word to go out that we want to exterminate the negro population, and the minister is the man who can straighten out that idea, if it ever occurs to their rebellious members." Margaret Sanger, on using black ministers to promote abortion

177

"The most merciful thing that a large family does to one of its infant members is to kill it." Margaret Sanger, Founder of Planned Parenthood

"As a society, I think we've been in denial about the risks of abortion both because of ideology, and because of economics. There are a lot of respectable doctors doing a lousy job." Dr. Warren Hern, author of *Abortion Practice*

"How is it that we have more oversight of women's hair salons and nail salons than we do over abortion clinics? " R. Seth Williams, Philadelphia District Attorney

"A high level of operator skill is at least as important in abortion as it is in any surgical endeavor. Abortion is a blind procedure that proceeds by touch, awareness of the nuances of sensations provided by instruments, honesty, and caution. Abortion, almost more than any other operation, demands experience to develop skill. Well trained, highly experienced, and reputable gynecologists found, to their dismay, that when abortions became legal and they began performing them, the complication rates were frequently high." Dr. Warren Hern, author of *Abortion Practice*

Conclusion

Since Roe v. Wade, there have been numerous studies on the after-effects of abortion. The combined results show a disturbing level of physical and psychological damage among millions of women. National policy on abortion is based on the premise that abortion is a safe procedure. If abortion is found to be unsafe, which it has been in many instances, the ruling on Roe v. Wade needs to be re-evaluated.

One of the basic principles of liberalism is the commitment to protect the most vulnerable members of the human community. Science proves that a baby, at any stage of development, is a human. Shouldn't Liberals want to protect these vulnerable humans? A difference in size, level of development, change in environment, or degree of dependency should not be relevant in establishing basic human rights. Should a newborn have fewer rights than an adult? Should older children have more rights than younger children? Where do you ethically draw the line? If being human is based on individual viability, then people who depend on medicines, or medical procedures, to stay alive, may then be technically non-human. A newborn cannot survive on its own. Does that make it a non-human?

Is it right to believe that strong and independent people deserve protection, while small and dependent people do not?

We've spent decades fighting against discrimination based on ethnicity and skin color, and have made great strides in its eradication. Unfortunately, we have taken a step backwards in the preservation of life. We now discriminate based on viability and level of physical development.

The more we understand about abortion, the more we realize it is anti-woman. The course of millions of women's lives has been forever altered at the direction of unscrupulous abortion providers who failed to educate these women about the risks. If anything deserves to be labeled "a war on women", this is it.

As with most political issues, education is the key to resolution. As more of the risks are exposed, mothers will be able to make more informed decisions, which will lessen the overall numbers of abortions.

If you are a woman who has had an abortion, and has ongoing issues as a result, you are not alone. There are a number of very good resources which provide comfort and support. Two of the best are www.silentnomoreawareness.org and www.afterabortion.com, which has almost two-and-a-half million posts.

Finally, I would like to thank my biological mother, wherever she may be, for not choosing abortion. Because of that unselfish decision, I have been able to live a fulfilling life, raised by two incredible people who were unable to have children of their own. There has never been a second of resentment. Even though we've never met, I love you with all my heart for the life you gave me. Please take comfort in knowing you did the right thing. God bless you.

CHAPTER TEN

The War on Women

The alleged "war on women" has to be one of the most ridiculous issues in the history of politics. Unfortunately, there are a number of gullible, uninformed voters who actually buy that nonsense. This chapter is for those of you who drank the Kool-Aid.

First of all, let me start by saying that there is no outright "war on women" by any political party in the United States. If there was, I'm afraid the Democrats would win hands-down. Their policies are the ones hurting women the most. Since the Democrats insisted on starting this argument, I will take the liberty of finishing it.

The Democrats love to manufacture issues when it starts getting close to election time. This is one of the more entertaining issues. I find it quite ironic that the party who is accusing the Republicans of waging a "war on women", has Bill Clinton as their flag-bearer. Can you imagine Hillary Clinton running for president in 2016, and her bringing up the "war on women?" For a political writer, that would be the best Christmas present ever.

Let's take a look at this mythical war and determine its validity, starting with President Obama. In at least three separate speeches, President Obama made the following statement, "Today, the average full-time working woman earns just seventy-seven cents for every dollar a man earns . . . in 2014, that's an embarrassment. It is wrong."

The president got two things right in that quote . . . it was wrong, by omission, and it is definitely an embarrassment to have politicians trying to manipulate women with phony issues. This leads me to two possible conclusions: either President Obama knows he is misrepresenting the facts, or he truly does not understand the issue. Neither answer is acceptable. Even many Democrats are holding their noses on this one. Here are the facts:

The Seventy-Seven Cent Myth

The seventy-seven cent figure is determined using Census Bureau figures, which take the average median income for men, minus the average median income for women, which leaves a pay gap of twenty-three cents. Using hourly wages, the gap drops to fourteen cents. No one disputes that there is a small wage gap. What we are not being told are the valid reasons why the wage gap exists.

Men and women are wired differently, and as such will often choose different career paths for a variety of reasons. It's these choices that create the wage disparity.

Women and men are paid based on skill level and production, not gender. Women with the same skill sets and productivity levels make just as much as men. If every employer got equal production and skill levels from women, at a twenty-three percent discount, all of the men in the world would be unemployed. Capitalism and the free market system will assure women of a commensurate wage.

Women generally have less work experience than men, and more women work part-time. Many women also leave the work force for extended periods to raise children, or on maternity leaves.

These women often chose jobs that pay less, but have more flexible hours in order to accommodate their lifestyle. Simply put, many women choose to have a more balanced life. Allowing women to make their own career choices can hardly be considered a "war on women."

Another reason men make more is because many jobs dominated by men have higher physical or economic risks. Those jobs pay more, but the cost of failure often includes injury, death or bankruptcy. Ninety-two percent of workplace fatalities in the U.S. are men. Men also work more hours than women. Still, The Bureau of Labor Statistics shows that unmarried women earn within four cents of men.

Also, more women are choosing not to enter into STEM (Science, Technology, Engineering, and Mathematics) careers. In 2000, women earned nineteen percent of the B.A. degrees given in engineering. In 2011, they only earned seventeen percent. Women earned twenty-eight percent of Computer Science B.A. degrees in 2000, which has dropped to eighteen percent as of 2011. So, although women have the talent, they are simply choosing other occupations.

Georgetown University did a survey on the economic value of various college majors. The survey showed that nine of the ten most lucrative majors were dominated by men. All ten of these majors were STEM disciplines (Science, Technology, Engineering, and Mathematics).

By contrast, nine of the ten least lucrative majors were dominated by women. These majors included social work, theater arts, studio arts, human services, early childhood education, counseling, psychology, and health and medical prep.

This gap will not disappear, because women will always have the choice to pursue careers that provide balance and flexibility, rather than pursuing a career for strictly monetary purposes.

The Democrats War on Women

The claims of a Republican "war on women" are based primarily on women's reproductive rights. Democrats support a "pro-choice" agenda. Their issue is that Republicans don't support taxpayer-funded abortion and birth-control pills. I say, "Hey, they're your choices, you should pay for them." If Democrats are really concerned about the well-being of women, why aren't they warning mothers about the risks of abortion? I don't know of a single instance where a pregnant mother was warned of the dangers of abortion. Despite a preponderance of evidence linking abortion to an increased risk of breast cancer, and myriad additional physical and psychological risks, Democrats and Democrat-supported abortionists fail to inform patients of the dangers. That's a war on women.

Come on, Democrats. Do you really think women are so shallow that subsidized birth control is at the top of their agendas? Mature women think about more than birth control. They are still paying high prices for gas. Their energy costs are continuing to increase. For the first time in their lives, women have seen a reduction in their discretionary income. Poverty among women is at a record high. The Democrats passed Obamacare, which most American women are against. Now, millions of women have a more expensive health plan, which is inferior to their previous plans, and thousands have lost their doctors. Millions more women will see increasing healthcare costs as the Obamacare mandates roll out. Many others will have their hours reduced at work by employers who can no longer afford the increased costs of insurance coverage for full-time employees under Obamacare. The Democrats don't seem to care as much about those issues. That is a war on women.

Since Obama took office, more than 5.5 million women have left the workforce. The labor-force participation rate for women has dropped from 60.8 percent to 58.5 percent, and unemployment among black women has risen from 9.2 percent to 10.1 percent.

Only thirty-nine percent of new jobs have gone to women since Obama took office. By contrast, sixty-five percent of new jobs went to women during George W. Bush's two terms. As of September 2014, a record 55,553,000 women were not participating in the labor force. The labor- force participation rate for women, as of September 2014, was 56.7 percent—the lowest it has been since September 1988. That is a war on women.

Barack Obama recently unveiled a new program called "My Brother's Keeper" that helps provide guidance and mentorship to young men of color. He has not unveiled any similar programs for women of color, or, for that matter, for any young women.

Democrats also want to take our guns away. How many thousands of women do you think carry a gun for self-defense? How many do you think will want to trade their guns for a rape whistle?

In April 2014, the Florida Senate passed legislation prohibiting Florida courts from considering certain provisions of foreign laws, including Islamic Sharia Law. This legislation, known as "American Laws for American Courts", was passed by the Republican majority. Every Democrat in the Florida Senate voted against it. Sharia Law is the single most anti-woman belief system in the world. Under Sharia, honor killings of wives and daughters are acceptable. Men can marry children and "consummate" the marriage when the child is less than ten years old. Stoning, flogging, and beating of women are commonplace. Women under Sharia have half the value of a man. To prove rape, a woman must have at least four male witnesses. Muslim women are forbidden to marry outside of their religion. In some countries, genital mutilation is also commonplace. That's a war on women.

The Florida Democrats are not alone. California's U.S. Representative, Democrat Maxine Waters, and several other members of Congress, have also come out in direct support of alternative laws, including Sharia Law. How can the Democrats accuse anyone of waging a "war on women" while condoning militant Islam?

Bill Clinton continues to be the unspoken leader of the Left. Let's see what Mr. Clinton has done to aid in the fight against the Republican war on women.

So far, the revered icon of the Democrat party has managed a sordid affair with an intern in the Oval Office, verified by DNA evidence. He has also been accused of sexual misconduct with Gennifer Flowers, Juanita Broaddrick, Paula Corbin, Kathleen Willey, Elizabeth Ward Gracen, Ellen Wellstone, Paula Jones, Carolyn Moffet, Sandra Allen James, Kathy Bradshaw, and Christy Zercher. Three of these situations held allegations of rape. There are literally dozens of additional rumored trysts.

How about Hillary Clinton? She spent years covering for Mr. Clinton's personal "war on women." Now, she seems to be the heir apparent as the next Democratic Party nominee for president. When it comes to protecting women, I have a story to relate about Hillary.

In 1975, Hillary Clinton defended a forty-one year-old man named Thomas Alfred Taylor, who had raped and brutalized a twelve-year-old girl, leaving her infertile, and in a coma for five days. During a taped interview in the mid-1980s, Clinton implied she knew Taylor was guilty, and used a legal technicality to plead him down to a lesser crime. On the tape, Clinton is heard chuckling as she recalls her courtroom strategy. I guess I missed the funny part of that story.

Republicans have also had their share of people who have had inappropriate conduct with women. The difference is that Republicans don't elevate their offenders to idol status after the misconduct. So, who's really waging the "war on women?"

TALKING POINTS

Climate Change

- No man-made warming has yet been detected that is distinct from naturally-occurring warming patterns. All empirical evidence suggests nature controls the climate, not man.

- The earth's temperature has fluctuated for thousands of years. Our current temperature is below the average temperature of the past 3000 years.

- In the 1970s the media and politicians were all on the bandwagon with the "science experts" who claimed we were well on our way to the next Ice Age, which was a hoax.

- The "evidence" for human-caused climate change cited by the alarmists is based on General Circulation Models, i.e. climate models, which have yet to be proven accurate. Not one of the thousands of climate models created accurately predicted our current seventeen-year span of zero temperature increase.

- Of the warming that has occurred since 1850, approximately seventy percent occurred prior to 1940. The claim that a post-World War II industrial build-up is responsible for carbon emissions that lead to global warming is baseless.

- Climate writer Russell Cook recently reported he had chronicled the broadcast transcripts for the *PBS News Hour*, with regard to global warming, over an eighteen-year period. During that period, there were approximately 400 instances where global warming was discussed. The program only mentioned evidence critical of global warming one percent of the time.

- An *NBC News* Special claimed that 2013 was a "year of extreme weather." It was actually an extremely calm weather year. There were only 771 tornadoes in 2013, the lowest number since 2000, and well below average (2011 had 1894 tornadoes and 2004 had 1820 tornadoes). The number of wild fires (40,306) were down from 2012 (67,774) and 2011 (74,126), and were the lowest reported numbers in over a decade. The number of 100-degree days in the U.S. was the lowest on record. And hurricanes saw one of the weakest years in recent history. The U.S. has not seen a category three, four, or five hurricane since 2005—the longest period since the Civil War.

- There were only seven weather and climate disasters in the U.S. in 2013, and all of them were in the central part of the country. This number was down from eleven in 2012 and fourteen in 2011. The Climate Extremes' Index from NOAA shows weather extremes were below average in 2013.

- The number of high temperature records in the U.S. dropped by approximately sixty percent from 2012 to 2013. For the first time in over a decade, the number of record-low temperatures exceeded the number of record-high temperatures.

- 2013 was only the 37th warmest year in the 119-year period of record. The five years with the most 100-degree days in the U.S. were 1930, 1934, 1936, 1954, and 1980. None of those periods were even in the last thirty years.

- Glaciers have been growing and receding for thousands of years. Scientists know of at least thirty-three separate periods when glaciers grew and receded. In many cases, reduction in ice and snow mass was actually due to lower precipitation levels, not global warming.

- In 1992, a petition was circulated by scientists informing the world of the false global warming narrative being portrayed by politicians and the media. It was signed by more than 4,000 scientists from 106 countries, including seventy-two Nobel Prize Winners

- Prior to the Kyoto Conference in 1997, a similar petition was signed by more than 15,000 scientists, most with advanced degrees, urging the U.S. Government to reject the Kyoto treaty. The scientists stated that the treaty was based on flawed ideas and was contrary to their research.

- Greenpeace co-founder Patrick Moore, testifying before the Senate Environmental and Public Works Committee, stated, "There is no scientific proof that human emissions of carbon dioxide are the dominant cause of the minor warming of the earth's atmosphere over the past 100 years." He also claimed the IPCC's probability figures for man-made global warming had been invented, and that the IPCC's reliance on computer models was futile.

- The latest NIPCC report, titled Climate Change Reconsidered II: Physical Science, concludes that "neither the rate nor the magnitude of the reported late twentieth century surface warming (1979 to 2000) lies outside normal natural variability, nor is it in any way unusual compared to earlier episodes in earth's history."

- In its review of the latest IPCC report (September, 2013), the NIPCC challenged the IPCC's claim of a ninety-five percent certainty that there is man-made global warming. The NIPCC found that the ninety-five percent certainty was based solely on a limited number of climate models that agreed with each other on man-made global warming, not actual observations.

The actual observations show no indication of human influence on global warming.

- Carbon dioxide accounts for less than .0004 (four ten-thousandths of one percent) of the earth's atmosphere, and only about three percent of that is produced by human activity.

- The only proven effect of rising carbon dioxide in the atmosphere is an increase in plant growth.

- Nine-hundred-thousand years of ice-core-temperature records and CO2 content records show that carbon dioxide increases follow increases in earth temperature, which is logical since oceans are the primary source of carbon dioxide. As the global climate cools, the oceans absorb more carbon dioxide. As the climate warms, the oceans release carbon dioxide. Thus, the alarmist claims that increasing CO2 levels *cause* global warming is totally false. Increased CO2 is the *result* of warming temperatures.

- It appears more likely that climate change is controlled by variations in solar magnetic activity and by periodic changes in ocean circulation. During the current 300-year recovery period from the Little Ice Age, temperature variations have correlated almost perfectly with fluctuations in solar activity. This correlation long predates the start of the industrial period.

- Global warming alarmism offers an excuse for governments to increase taxes and create taxpayer-funded green energy projects. The greater the fear of a climate catastrophe, the more amenable people will be to accepting higher taxes and higher energy costs.

The Race Card

- In both principle and practice, the Republican Party has a far better track record than the Democrats when it comes to race.

- Democrats have passed legislation, such as a broken welfare system, that rewards poor mothers for having children out-of-wedlock and punishes them for being married. In 1965, over seventy-six percent of black children were born to married women. Today, seventy-three percent of black children are born out of wedlock, and sixty-seven percent live in single-parent homes.

- Prior to the programs of the Great Society, black teenage pregnancies had been decreasing, poverty and dependency were declining, and income among blacks was increasing in both absolute and relative terms compared to white income. Prior to the 1960s, the unemployment rate for black teenagers was under ten percent. Today, black teen unemployment is almost forty percent. Since the 1970s, marriage in the African-American community is down by thirty-four percent, double the national average.

- The Republican Party was founded primarily to oppose slavery and it was the Republicans who eventually abolished slavery.

- Nathan Bedford Forrest, a Democrat, founded the Ku Klux Klan, as an extension of the Southern Democrat Party. The

Klan's objective was to terrorize and suppress African-Americans and their supporters. Virtually all lynchings of blacks took place in regions controlled by Democrats.

- Abraham Lincoln was a Republican. Unfortunately his Vice-President, Andrew Johnson, was a Democrat. Johnson, along with the Southern Democrats, were against civil rights for the freed slaves and vigorously fought against them after Lincoln's assassination.

- It was the Democrat Party that instituted the Jim Crow Laws, which assured blacks would remain second-class citizens.

- It was Republican Dwight Eisenhower who pushed to pass the Civil Rights Act of 1957, and sent troops to Arkansas to desegregate the schools.

- On July 2, 1964, Congress enacted the Civil Rights Act of 1964. It was actually supported by a larger percentage of Republicans than Democrats in both the House and the Senate. In the House, eighty percent of the Republicans voted in favor of the Act, compared to sixty-three percent of the Democrats. The Senate vote was similar with eighty-two percent of Republicans and sixty-nine percent of Democrats voting in favor.

- Overall, there were twenty-six major civil rights votes from 1933 through the civil rights' period of the 1960s. The Republicans voted in favor of civil rights over ninety-five percent of the time. During that same period, Democrats voted *against* civil rights *eighty percent of the time.*

- There is a disparity in media coverage on crime, depending upon the race of the respective victims and perpetrators.

- Whites outnumber blacks by a five-to-one margin in population, yet blacks commit eight times more crimes against whites.

- Affirmative Action is fundamentally racist. It is based on the assumption that minorities are incapable of competing with whites. Affirmative Action is really racial preference, and racial preferences often reinforce stereotypes of inequality and special treatment, and tarnish the legitimacy of one's achievements.

- A 2013 *Washington Post/ABC News* poll found that seventy-six percent of Americans, from all races and political affiliations, opposed race-based college admissions.

- Prior to the election of Barack Obama as President in 2008, we were making significant progress toward living in a post-racial America. At that time, an *NBC News/Wall Street Journal* poll showed that seventy-nine percent of whites and sixty-three percent of blacks held a favorable opinion of race relations. The same poll, taken four and a half years into Obama's presidency, found that those with a favorable opinion had dropped to fifty-two percent among whites and thirty-eight percent among blacks: a twenty-seven point and twenty-five point drop, respectively. Several decades of progress had been erased in four-and-a-half years. And the gap has continued to widen.

- Attorney General Eric Holder refused to prosecute the Black Panther members because they were black. Holder refers to blacks, including the Black Panthers, as "my people." As the U.S. Attorney General, shouldn't everyone in America be "his people?"

Gun Control

- Based on historical data, gun control is more likely to escalate violent crime, including murder. States and counties with the strictest gun laws tend to have higher rates of overall crime, including gun crime.

- Gun control only affects the law-abiding citizens. Criminals usually get their guns illegally, by theft, black market purchase, or straw purchase.

- Historically, murder rates have increased in every area that has banned all guns, or handguns.

- Almost all mass-shootings have taken place in "gun-free" zones. Mass killers may be mentally unstable, but they know enough to carry out their atrocities in areas that are generally devoid of armed citizens.

- Using the latest available statistics, the media reports that more than 32,000 Americans are killed by gun violence every year. What most fail to report is that sixty-one percent of those deaths were suicides, and twenty-eight percent were gang-related. An additional three percent were accidental shootings, two percent were self-defense, and six percent were classified as "other."

- The rate of firearm homicide deaths in the U.S. is 3.6 per 100,000 people, which puts the United States in the middle of all countries worldwide. Honduras was the highest at 68.4 per 100,000 people.

- If the gang-related gun homicides were excluded from the U.S. total, we would actually rank below Switzerland, which is well below one per 100,000.

- In 1960, there were a total of approximately 77.5 million privately-owned guns in the United States, with a total population of about 179 million people. Based on those figures, there was one gun for every 2.31 people. The murder rate in 1960 was 5.1 per 100,000 people. In 2012, the number of privately-owned guns had increased to an estimated 333 million, based on estimates from the Bureau of Alcohol Tobacco and Firearms. The U.S. population had increased to approximately 316 million people. This puts the current gun ownership ratio at just over one per person, more than double the 1960 ratio. Yet, the murder rate in 2012 was only 4.7 per 100,000 people.

- When the 1994 Federal Assault Weapons Ban expired in 2004, the murder rate was 5.5 per 100,000. If assault weapons play such a key role in the murder rate, why has the murder rate declined since the expiration of the ban?

- Overall, the statistics continue to show that the cities and states with the strictest gun control laws have the most gun violence. In states that have right-to-carry laws, the murder rate is twenty-eight percent lower than in the states that don't. Violent crime is twenty-four percent lower.

- In 1977, a handgun ban went into effect in Washington, D.C. The ban also included a requirement that other firearms be kept unloaded and dis-assembled. Since the ban took effect, there has only been one year that the murder rate fell below pre-ban levels. In fact, D.C. ranked among the top four major cities in the U.S. for the highest annual murder rate nineteen times, earning the nickname "Murder Capital."

- Massachusetts passed strict gun laws in 1998, a year in which there were sixty-five gun homicides statewide. From 1998 to 2011, armed robbery rose 20.7 percent, and aggravated assaults rose 26.7 percent. In 2011, there were 122 gun homicides in Massachusetts. While the overall murder rate for the country was falling, Massachusetts was climbing.

- Ten cities alone accounted for approximately twelve percent of the total U.S. gun homicides. They all share one thing in common: they are all Democrat-controlled cities with generally strict gun laws. By comparison, Utah, which the Brady Campaign determined to have the least gun control, had a gun homicide rate of less than one percent.

- In Illinois, the concealed carry ban was lifted effective January 2014. Not surprisingly, the murder rate in Chicago plummeted. Through August 2014, the murder rate was down nine percent from the same period in 2013, and twenty-seven percent from 2012.

- When criminals don't feel threatened by armed citizens, it also changes the dynamics of their crimes. In the U.K., nearly half of all burglaries are committed while the victim is home, compared to only thirteen percent of burglaries in the United States that are committed while the victim is home.

- There have been literally millions of instances of defensive gun use, which prevented untold numbers of violent crimes, including murder, rape, and armed robbery. These are crimes that would not have been prevented if the potential victims had not been armed. It's difficult to arrive at an estimate of defensive-gun-use incidents in the United States, but published reports give estimates of between 108,000 and 3.6 million annually.

- In a study done by the National Crime Survey, robberies succeed eighty-eight percent of the time, and victims are injured twenty-five percent of the time, when a victim does not defend himself. However, when the victim defends himself with a gun, the robbery success rate drops to thirty percent and the victim injury rate drops to seventeen percent.

- Of the most prolific mass-murders in U.S. history, the majority did not use a gun.

- Gun control proponents should redirect their efforts to the person using the gun, not the gun itself. Mental illness is the primary cause of mass murders.

Immigration

- The majority of Americans do not favor amnesty or increased immigration. A Gallup Poll taken in June 2014, showed that forty-one percent of adults in the U.S. want to see immigration decreased, while only twenty-two percent said they would like to see immigration increased.

- The immigrants who came through Ellis Island were far different than those today. The immigrants who came through Ellis Island did not receive government assistance. There was no welfare state. They all brought important skills with them, those of tailors, master carpenters, stone masons, bricklayers, artisans, all of which enhanced the American economy. They either made it on their own, or relied on family or friends until they could. About seventy percent of those immigrants were men in their prime. They learned English and adopted the American culture.

- The problems resulting from illegal immigration include increased crime, overcrowded schools, increased healthcare costs, lower wages, higher insurance costs, higher taxes, voter fraud, and cultural degradation. Dozens of hospitals have had to close because immigrants with no insurance have exhausted the resources, without the ability to compensate for services received.

- Fewer than six percent of the legal immigrants in 2009 were admitted because they possessed skills which were deemed essential to the U.S. economy.

- A report by the Center for Immigration Studies, released in 2014, found that almost all of the net employment growth in the United States since 2000 has gone to immigrants, both legal and illegal. The report shows that 127,000 fewer working-age natives held jobs in the first quarter of 2014 than in 2000. In contrast, the number of immigrants with a job had increased by 5.7 million in the same period.

- Currently, many other western nations are restricting immigration due to the same issues we are facing.

- A recent study by the Heritage Foundation found that the average household headed by an illegal immigrant receives about $24,721 in government benefits and services, while only paying about $10,334 in taxes, for a net fiscal deficit of $14,387 per household, based on all skill and educational levels. Those households headed by an illegal immigrant without a high school diploma, receive $20,485 more in benefits and services per year than they pay in taxes.

- Amnesty would increase the average annual tax deficit by fifty-five percent for former illegal immigrants , while allowing them access to more than eighty means-tested welfare programs. Once amnesty has been fully implemented, the average benefits and services to former illegal immigrant households would increase to about $43,900, with taxes paid only being about $16,000 per year, for a fiscal deficit of $27,900 per year per household.

- If amnesty is enacted, the average illegal immigrant would receive about $582,000 more in benefits and services over his lifetime than he pays in taxes, based on 2010 dollars.

- Proponents of amnesty argue that it would help make Social Security solvent, because the illegal immigrants would pay more in FICA taxes after amnesty. However, based on current wage levels, the average illegal immigrant would only be paying about $3,700 per year in FICA taxes while receiving net benefits of about $25,000 per year.

- The Heritage Foundation estimates the national fiscal deficit for illegal immigrant labor to be about $55 billion. The Federation of Americans for Immigration Reform estimates the deficit is approximately $99 billion.

- According to a report by the Treasury Department's inspector general, illegal immigrants fraudulently received $4.2 billion in child-support tax credits in 2010, increasing to an estimated $7.4 billion in 2012.

- Immigrant use of the medical system, and subsequent non-payment for services, has already forced more than eighty hospitals to close their doors in California alone.

- In 1980, there were fewer than 9,000 criminal aliens in our state and federal prisons. As of 2009, there were 295,959 criminal aliens incarcerated in state prisons and local jails in the United States. Of these, 204,136 were in local jails and 91,823 were in state prisons. An additional 55,000 were incarcerated in federal prisons.

- In 2009, the cost to incarcerate a single criminal alien was $34,448 per year in California, and $29,523 per year in New York. The average cost nationwide was $12,520 per year.

- From 2008 to 2012, 143,000 criminal aliens were arrested and jailed in Texas alone. They were charged with 447,000 offenses, including more than 5,000 rapes and 2,000 murders. That's in one state.

- An in-depth study done by the Violent Crimes Institute, covering the period from January 1999 through April 2006, arrived at a conservative estimate of 240,000 illegal immigrant sex offenders in the U.S. at that time. Of the 1500 sex offenders in the study, each averaged four victims. The crimes committed included rape, sexual homicides, and child molestation. Based on that study, there were an estimated 960,000 sex crimes committed by illegal aliens throughout the U.S. during that eighty-eight month period. That equates to 363 sex crimes per day.

- A report released in March 2010, by the Department of Justice National Security Division, showed that international terrorism investigations had led to the convictions of 399 individuals since September 11, 2001. Of these, 173 individuals were, at the time of charging, aliens in the U.S. with or without legal immigration status.

- As immigration has increased over the last few decades, we have seen outbreaks of diseases in America that used to be confined to third-world countries.

- American workers lose an estimated $405 billion due to companies using lower cost legal and illegal foreign workers. This equates to about $2800 per American worker per year.

- A study done by the Pew Hispanic Center found that, of the Mexican immigrants who have been in the U.S. for less than two years, only five percent were unemployed in Mexico prior to leaving for the U.S.

- When we bring in labor from other countries, we aren't simply bringing in workers. We are bringing in differing cultures, politics, languages, belief systems, religions, preferences, etc. It's much more complicated than we are led to believe.

Minimum Wage

- Since its inception in 1938, the federal minimum wage has been increased twenty-four times, and has been proven to be completely ineffective at reducing poverty.

- When poll respondents were asked if they would vote for the minimum-wage increase, knowing that a number of people would lose their jobs, fifty-seven percent opposed the increase and only thirty-eight percent said they would vote for it.

- The importance of a minimum-wage job is to provide skills and training, which in turn makes the employee more productive and gives them the ability to command higher pay in the future. Nearly two-thirds of minimum wage workers receive a pay increase within one year.

- Minimum-wage earners are generally new to the job market, often teenagers with little or no skills, immigrants, unskilled older workers, workers with disabilities, and people without a high school diploma. Over half of the people in America started their careers making within a dollar of the minimum wage.

- According to the Bureau of Labor Statistics, there were approximately 144 million people employed in the United States in 2013. Only 2.3 percent of these workers earned at or below minimum wage (approximately 3.3 million workers). Of this group, just over half (50.4 percent or 1.663 million) were only twenty-four years of age or younger. Another 13.2 percent (436,000) were between 25-29 years of age. Workers over the age of thirty making minimum wage only accounted for 0.8 percent of the total U.S. workforce.

- Families with a single parent working full-time at minimum wage, which Democrats often cite as being a major issue, accounts for only four percent of minimum-wage workers (approximately 132,000).

- The President claims raising the minimum wage from $7.25 per hour to $10.10 per hour will lift a million full-time minimum-wage workers out of poverty. They are already out of poverty. A person who makes the current minimum wage of $7.25 per hour will make $15,080 per year working full-time, which is $3,410 over the poverty limit. This does not include any tips, overtime, or commissions.

- There have been eight studies done since 1995 that examined the impact of minimum-wage increases on poverty. All but one found that prior minimum-wage increases had no effect on poverty. These same studies also concluded that while some poverty-level , low-skilled workers did see an increase in income, many other low-skilled workers either lost their jobs or suffered a reduction in hours, leading to reduced income, which resulted in increased poverty.

- The only real solution to reducing poverty is through job creation.

- The primary finding of studies done since the minimum wage was first established, is that minimum-wage increases tend to reduce employment. The findings also show that the higher the minimum-wage increase, relative to competitive-market wage levels, the greater the loss of jobs.

- In a struggling economy, employers will not hire workers whose production level is below the wages being paid. If the minimum wage is raised to $10.10 per hour, then those workers whose labor brings in less than that to the business are no longer a good investment.

- Economists have estimated that a ten-percent increase in labor costs will result in a workforce reduction of about three percent. If that statement holds true, then the current proposed minimum-wage hike (39.3%) would equate to a workforce reduction of at least twelve percent of those making minimum wage. Studies have also found that a ten-percent minimum-wage increase would also raise food prices by up to four percent.

- The preponderance of evidence has proven that minimum-wage laws are harmful to low-skilled workers, youth, immigrants, the disabled, and the economy in general.

- The only successes attributable to prior minimum-wage increases are that of the unions and the Democrats, who have successfully parlayed this issue into higher union revenues, increased negotiating power, and ultimately, higher campaign contributions.

- A recent poll, taken of voters who were apprised of the potential job losses, showed that sixty-eight percent of Republicans, fifty-three percent of Independents , and fifty percent of Democrats would oppose a minimum wage increase under those circumstances.

Unemployment

- Despite all of our current technology and sophisticated reporting capabilities, we are still using the same data-collection method we used in 1940: phone surveys of 60,000 people. It seems unlikely that the Bureau of Labor Statistics could arrive at accurate numbers by surveying fewer than one-tenth of one percent of the labor force.

- The unemployment number reported by the mainstream media is virtually always the U-3 number. This is not an accurate reflection of unemployment because it omits millions of discouraged workers, marginally-attached workers, and those employed part-time for economic reasons.

- The U-6 number provides the most accurate accounting of the unemployment picture.

- At the same time the mainstream media was reporting positive job creation trends in 2014, the labor force participation rate was at its lowest level in thirty-six years. It had dropped from 65.5 percent to 62.7 percent since Obama took office. That is not a good statistic if you intend to brag about job creation.

- As of June 2014, there were 92,584,000 people not in the workforce, an all-time record. That number represents an increase of more than eleven million since January 2009.

- The labor-force participation rate for whites has dropped from 65.9 percent to 62.8 percent, with more than seven million whites leaving the work force.

- The black labor-force participation rate is down from 63.4 percent to 61.7 percent. More than one-and-a-half-million blacks have left the work force.

- Black female unemployment is actually much worse since Obama took office, jumping from 9.2 percent 10.6 percent as of August 2014, despite the number leaving the workforce. At the same time, black teenage unemployment was at 32.8 percent.

- Among Hispanics, the labor force participation rate has dropped from 67.5 percent to 65.9 percent. More than two-and-a-half-million Hispanics have left the work force.

- When Barack Obama took office, the labor-force participation rate was 65.5 percent. If that rate had remained constant, the June U-3 unemployment rate would have been 10.3 percent, and the U-6 rate would have been in the high teens.

- In June 2014, the number of people taking part-time jobs, because they couldn't find full-time jobs, increased by 275,000. So, out of the 288,000 jobs created in June, 275,000 were part-time.

- A total of 523,000 full-time jobs were lost in June 2014. At the same time, the number of people working part-time for non-economic reasons rose by 840,000, which is the largest increase since 1993.

- As of September 2014, a record 55,553,000 women were not participating in the labor force. The labor-force participation rate for women, as of September 2014, was 56.7 percent, the lowest it has been since September 1988.

- Virtually, all of the drop in the U-3 unemployment rate since 2009 is the result of the drop in the labor-force participation rate. There is no significant job creation. The number is going down because so many people have quit looking for work and are no longer counted. The actual U-6 unemployment rate for June was 12.1 percent, a far cry from the 6.1 percent the media reported. Even at the questionable 6.1 percent figure, Obama is still well-behind George W. Bush, whose average unemployment rate, during his eight years in office, was 5.3 percent. In his first five years, Obama averaged 8.6 percent.

Income Inequality

- Income inequality is a fact of life. Most Americans understand that income disparity is healthy in a free-market society. Those who produce more, by virtue of their own ideas and actions, earn the wealth they create, and deserve to keep it.

- We all make choices throughout our lives that determine the outcome of our future financial situation. Differences in physical capabilities, work ethic, intellectual levels, drive, and ambition, are all factors that will determine our future prosperity. As we get older, other factors come into play: education, skill level, career choice, family situations, and other interests that will affect our earnings.

- Of the top 400 income-earners in the United States during the last forty years, only fifteen percent were able to stay in the top 400 for longer than two years. The media would like us to think that the rich stay rich and the poor stay poor, which is obviously not the case.

- If you use all income and tax liability figures, and account for the demographic disparities in the Census Bureau numbers, income inequality actually declined sixty-eight percent between 1983 and 2009.

- A CBO report, released in October 2011, showed that family income, including benefits, on average, experienced a sixty-two percent gain above inflation from 1979 to 2007. All five quintiles experienced gains.

- Census Bureau data is marred by four problems that lead to a substantial overstatement of income inequality. The problems are as follows:

  1. Conventional census income figures are incomplete and omit many types of cash and non-cash income.

  2. Conventional census figures do not factor in the equalizing effects of taxation.

  3. Census Bureau quintiles do not contain equal numbers of persons, which greatly magnifies the apparent level of income inequality.

  4. The Census Bureau numbers fail to recognize the huge disparity in the number of hours worked in each quintile.

  Any one of these four issues would have a significant impact on income-disparity calculations. Combined, they completely distort the true income-inequality picture.

- Using conventional Census Bureau figures, the top quintile is shown as receiving about $14.00 in income for every $1.00 in the bottom quintile. However, once all incomes are counted, and taxes are considered, the ratio drops to about $8.00 for every $1.00 of income. If you then adjust the quintiles to contain equal numbers of persons, the ratio of incomes between the top and bottom quintiles drops to just over $4.00 to $1.00, a large portion of which is due to the disparity in total work hours. If the adults in both quintiles worked the same number of hours, the final income-disparity gap would fall to just over $3.00 for the top quintile, compared to $1.00 for the bottom quintile, which just about wipes out the inequality narrative.

- Of the six million jobs created during Obama's "recovery", the vast majority have been low-wage and part-time jobs. The percentage of part-time workers is up forty-three percent. The number of people on food stamps has increased by almost fifty percent. During his first five years in office, the average payroll for American workers, measured in inflation-adjusted dollars, only increased 0.3 percent. All of these factors have contributed to a reduction in income for the bottom quintile.

- Of the forty-six million people classified as "poverty level" by the Census Bureau, only a small percentage would be considered destitute. While real material hardship does occur, the scope and severity of poverty in America has been greatly exaggerated by the media and the left.

- The cities with the highest levels of income inequality are all cities controlled by Democrats, all of which voted overwhelmingly to re-elect Obama, and his policies, in 2012. Only three Republican cities were in the top fifty, the highest being Phoenix at number thirty-eight.

- The Democrat solution to reducing income inequality involves a redistribution of income through increases in government assistance and higher taxes. This "solution" will discourage hiring and investment, and will depress economic growth and opportunity.

Abortion

- Thirty years ago, those who held a pro-life view were in the minority. However, a Gallup Poll taken in May 2009 showed that, for the first time, a significantly greater percentage of Americans identified themselves as pro-life.

- A Gallup Poll released in May 2014 revealed that fifty-nine percent felt abortion should either always be illegal, or illegal except in the case of rape, incest, or life of the mother. They also supported overturning Roe v. Wade. A *CNN* poll taken two months earlier showed identical results.

- Both pre-abortive and post-abortive women are regularly misled by clinic counselors, and never properly informed of the potential dangers, such as an increased risk of future breast cancer. This lack of honesty on the part of the abortion industry may indicate that they have less regard for women's health than they do money and politics.

- Virtually all scientists agree, and science documents, the fact that life begins at conception.

- Human embryos develop at an incredibly rapid pace. The brain and heart begin forming only two weeks after conception, usually before the mother even realizes she is pregnant. At about twenty-two days after conception, that heart begins to circulate its own blood, different than that of the mother, and its heartbeat can be detected on ultrasound. At six weeks, the child's eyes, nose, mouth, and tongue have formed. Brain activity can be detected at six to seven weeks. By the end of the eighth week, the child has developed all of its organs and bodily structures. By the tenth week, the child can move its body.

- Most people don't understand the full extent of Roe v. Wade. It granted a virtually unlimited right to abortion under which *any* abortion can be justified. The court ruled that abortion must be permitted for *any reason* a woman chooses until viability. After viability is reached, an abortion must still be permitted if an abortion doctor deems the abortion necessary to protect a woman's "health." The definition of "health" was defined in Doe v. Bolton as "all factors- physical, emotional, psychological, familial, and the woman's age, relevant to the well-being of the patient." In other words, the court created the right to abort a child at any time, even past the point of viability, for "emotional" reasons. This ruling basically granted absolute power to the abortion doctors.

- Norma McCorvey (Jane Roe) never had an abortion, and later became a pro-life advocate. Think about that. The plaintiff in Roe v. Wade—the most famous abortion case in history— never had an abortion, and is now a pro-life advocate.

- Currently, a majority of Americans support overturning Roe v. Wade, which would not make abortion illegal, but would simply put the issue of abortion in the hands of the individual state's representatives, which are more likely to represent the will of the people.

- Despite numerous findings to the contrary, the abortion industry has continued to deny and censor any studies which indicate a correlation between abortion and breast cancer risk. What they do report are individual studies, usually done by pro-abortion researchers and institutions, showing no link between abortion and breast cancer, although they do state that "research is continuing."

- There have been dozens of studies done that have found a cancer link to abortion. In 1996, Joel Brind, a professor of Biology and Endocrinology at Baruch College, released a report which combined the results of twenty-three separate studies that indicated at least a thirty-percent higher risk of breast cancer for women having had an abortion.

- Another report, released in 2013, included thirty-six studies from fourteen provinces in China. Annual abortions in China exceed eight million, with 400 abortions for every 1000 live births. The report showed the risk of breast cancer increased by forty-four percent with one abortion, seventy-six percent with two abortions, and eighty-nine percent with three abortions. This is the most extensive study to-date and, unlike some of the studies done in the United States, the Chinese have no motivation to manipulate or censor their findings.

- There have been over fifty-five million abortions performed in the United States since Roe v. Wade. If you take the overall risk of breast cancer among women to be approximately ten percent and then increase that risk by the forty-four percent reported in the Chinese study, you end up with an additional 4.4% of the women who have had an abortion that will likely end up getting cancer. If we then take just the fifty-three percent of the women who have had one abortion since Roe v. Wade (forty-seven percent had multiple abortions), we get a total of 29.15 million women. We can assume that an additional 4.4 % of those women got cancer who otherwise would not have gotten it, which brings us to a total 1,282,600 women developing cancer as a direct result of having had an abortion. At a conservative mortality rate of fifteen percent, which is lower than the historic mortality rate, you arrive at a total of more than 192,000 additional breast cancer deaths since 1973 as a result of having had a single abortion, let alone multiple abortions. That's a far cry from the zero risk stated by Planned Parenthood.

- In addition to an increased risk of breast cancer, there are a number of other risks that women face by having an abortion. The most common issues include uterine damage, pelvic inflammatory disease, future ectopic pregnancies, increased rate of pre-term birth in future pregnancies, infertility, placental abruption, infection, psychological and emotional trauma, and death.

- Women who have undergone post-abortion counseling have reported over 100 major reactions to abortion. Among the most frequently reported are: severe depression, loss of self-esteem, grief, self-destructive behavior, sleep disorders, sexual dysfunction, difficulty forming relationships, anxiety attacks, increased tendency towards violence, alcohol or drug abuse, eating disorders, social regression, suicidal thoughts or tendencies, and difficulty bonding with later children.

- In a survey of 100 women suffering from post-abortion trauma, eighty percent expressed feelings of self-hatred, and sixty percent reported suicidal ideation, with twenty-eight percent actually attempting suicide. In the same study, forty-nine percent reported drug abuse and thirty-nine percent began to use, or increased, their use of alcohol. Of these, fourteen percent described themselves as "addicted."

- Pre-term birth (PTB) is the leading cause of neonatal death in the United States. It accounts for literally hundreds of thousands of deaths. There are 135 studies from around the world that link PTB to prior abortions. The pre-term birth rate in the United States prior to Roe v. Wade was about six percent. The PTB rate is now almost thirteen percent.

- The Centers for Disease Control released a report showing a dramatic increase in ectopic pregnancies, as a result of pelvic inflammatory disease, that closely paralleled the increase in abortions. Also, approximately two percent of all first-trimester surgical abortions result in a perforated uterus.

- Approximately two percent of all first-trimester surgical abortions result in a perforated uterus. And according to an article published in *American Journal of Obstetrics and Gynecology*, "approximately 2% to 10% of medical abortion patients will require surgical intervention.

War on Women

- Women and men are paid based on skill level and production, not gender. Women with the same skill sets and productivity levels make just as much as men.

- The Bureau of Labor Statistics shows that unmarried women earn within four cents of men.

- Despite a preponderance of evidence linking abortion to an increased risk of breast cancer, and a myriad of additional physical and psychological risks, Democrats and Democrat-supported abortionists fail to inform patients of the dangers.

- Mature women think about more than birth control. They are still paying high prices for gas. Energy costs are continuing to increase. For the first time in their lives, women have seen a reduction in their discretionary income. Poverty among women is at a record high. The Democrats passed Obamacare, which most American women are against. Now, millions of women have a more expensive health plan, which is inferior to their previous plans, and thousands have lost their doctors. Millions more women will see increasing healthcare costs as the Obamacare mandates roll out. Many others will have their hours reduced at work.

- Since Obama took office, more than 5.5 million women have left the workforce. The labor-force participation rate for women has dropped from 60.8 percent to 58.5 percent, and unemployment among black women has risen from 9.2 percent to 10.1 percent.

- Only thirty-nine percent of new jobs have gone to women since Obama took office. By contrast, sixty-five percent of new jobs went to women during George W. Bush's two terms.

- As of September 2014, a record 55,553,000 women were not participating in the labor force. The labor-force participation rate for women, as of September 2014, was 56.7 percent, the lowest it has been since September 1988.

- In April 2014, the Florida Senate passed legislation prohibiting Florida courts from considering certain provisions of foreign laws, including Islamic Sharia Law. This legislation, known as "American Laws for American Courts", was passed by the Republican majority. Every Democrat in the Florida Senate voted against it.

- Bill Clinton, the revered icon of the Democrat party, has been accused of sexual misconduct with numerous women, including three allegations of rape. Apparently, that type of behavior falls within acceptable guidelines in the Democrat party.

- In 1975, Hillary Clinton defended a forty-one year-old man named Thomas Alfred Taylor, who had raped and brutalized a twelve-year-old girl, leaving her infertile, and in a coma for five days. During a taped interview in the mid-1980s, Clinton implied she knew Taylor was guilty, and used a legal technicality to plead him down to a lesser crime. On the tape, Clinton is heard chuckling as she recalls her victory.

APPENDIX

Chapter One

Rayne, Sierra. "Reagan vs. Obama: It's Not Even Close." *American Thinker*. 12 August 2013. Print

Marcus, Lloyd. "Selling Conservatism To Minorities." *American Thinker*. 23 November 2013. Print

Gose, Ben. "Charity's Political Divide, Republicans Give A Bigger Share To Charity (Democrats Don't)." *The Chronicle Of Philanthropy*. 23 November 2006. Print

"What Politicians Give." *Free Money Finance*. September 2008. Print.

Walker, Bruce. "Gallup Poll Of Trust Shows Conservative America." *American Thinker*. 24 June 2014. Print

McQuillan, Karin. "Who The Democrats Really Are." *American Thinker*. 12 December 2013. Print

"Liberal vs. Conservative Values." NewsBasics.com. 2010.

United States Department Of Agriculture, Food and Nutrition Service. "Supplemental Nutrition Assistance Program. 6 June 2014. Print

Walker, Bruce. "We Are The Majority." *American Thinker*. 10 November 2013. Print

National Platform Plank, Conservative Party USA. New Orleans. July 2010. Print.

"Conservative vs. Liberal Beliefs." *Student News Daily*. 2013. Print.

United States Department Of Agriculture, Food and Nutrition Service. "Supplemental Nutrition Assistance Program. 6 June 2014. Print

United States Census Bureau. "Time Series: Seasonally Adjusted Home Ownership Rate." June 2014. Print.

United States Bureau of Labor Statistics. "Consumer Price Index—All Urban Consumers." June 2014. Print.

Cooper, Elise. "John F. Kennedy: Conservative?" *American Thinker*. 22 November 2013. Print

Brooks, David. "The Conservative Mind." *New York Times*. New York. 25 September, 2012. Print

Sowell, Thomas. "The Mindset Of The Left." *Jewish World Review*. 25 June 2013. Print

Sowell, Thomas. "The Mindset Of The Left: Part Two." *Jewish World Review*. 3 July 2013. Print

Sowell, Thomas. "The Mindset Of The Left: Part Three." *Jewish World Review*. 4 July 2013. Print

Sowell, Thomas. "The Mindset Of The Left: Part Four." *Jewish World Review*. 5 July 2013. Print

"Democrat Politicians Stingy On Charitable Giving." *IUSB Vision*. 30 December 2010. Walker, Bruce. "Abortion Polls And Hidden Conservatism." *American Thinker*. 27 May 2014. Print

Kristof, Nicholas D. "Bleeding Heart Tightwads." *New York Times*. 20 December 2008. Print

2012 Democratic National Platform, *Moving America Forward*. 2012. Print.

Chapter Two

Singer, Fred. "The Coming Paradigm On Climate." *American Thinker*. 27 March 2014. Print

Rice, Doyle. "It Was March Misery In Frigid Northern, Eastern USA." *USA Today*. 29 March 2014. Print

Battig, Charles. "The Denier Mantle Moves On." *American Thinker*. 28 March 2014. Print

Meredith, Charlotte. "100 Reasons Why Climate Change Is Natural." *Daily Express*. 20 November 2012. Print

Urban Heat Island Effect. Theoretical and Applied Climatology. Paper. 27 February 2014. Print.

Greenfield, Daniel. "Obama Blew $120 Billion On Global Warming." *Frontpage Magazine*. 12 March 2014. Print

Amos, Jonathan. "Arctic Summers Ice-Free 'By 2013'." *BBC News*. San Francisco. 2007. Print.

Gore, Al. "An Inconvenient Truth." Documentary Film. 2006.

Cook, Russell. "Smearing Climate Skeptics." *American Thinker*. 27 March 2014. Print

White, Marianne. "Frightening Projection For Arctic Melt." *Canwest News Service*. 1 November 2007. Print

Lewis, Nicholas and Crok, Marcel. "Oversensitive: How The IPCC Hid The Good News On Global Warming." The Global Warming Policy Foundation. 2014. Print.

Solomon, Lawrence. "How The Global Warming Cult Took Control Of Wikipedia." *National Post*. 22 December 2009. Print

Seitz, Frederick. "A Major Deception On Global Warming." *Wall Street Journal*. 12 June 1996. Print

Singer, Fred. "Coverup In The Greenhouse?" *Wall Street Journal*. 11 July 1996. Print

Sussman, Brian. "Global Warming's Reckless Rhetoric." *American Thinker*. 17 April 2012. Print

United States Environmental Protection Agency, "Climate Change and Health Effects." http://www.epa.gov/climatechange/downloads/climate_Change_Health.pdf.

Murphy, Paul Austin. "Wikipedia On Global Warming." *American Thinker*. 11 March 2014. Print

Sussman, Brian. "The Real Climate Deniers." *American Thinker*. 16 December 2008. Print

Battig, Charles. "The Dead Parrot Of Man-Made Climate Change." *American Thinker*. 12 March 2014. Print

Hayward, Steven F. "From Cancun To Kyoto." *National Review Online*. 8 December 2010. Print

The Kyoto Protocol, To The United Nations Framework Convention on Climate Change. Kyoto, Japan. 1997.

Houts, Douglas. "More Than 15,000 Scientists Protest Kyoto Accord; Speak Out Against Global Warming Myth." *Capitalism Magazine*. 12 May 1998. Print

Robinson, Arthur B. and Zachary W. Robinson. "Science Has Spoken: Global warming Is A Myth." *The Wall Street Journal*. 4 December 1997. Print

Michaels, Patrick J. and Knappenberger, Paul C. "Climate Insensitivity: What The IPCC Knew But Didn't Tell Us." *Global Science Report*. Center For The Study Of Science. 5 March 2014. Print

Carter, Prof. Robert M. "Global Warming: Ten Facts And Ten Myths On Climate Change." *GlobalResearch*. 15 January 2014. Print

Sowell, Thomas. "Global Warming Swindle: Hysterics Exposed." *Creators Syndicate*. 15 March 2007. Print

Kreutzer, David and Katie Tubb. "Global Warming Alarmists Pick And Choose Data To Support Theory." Heritage Foundation. 11 January 2013. Print

"Greenpeace Co-Founder Tells Truth About Climate Change." Investors.com. 27 February 2014

"Greenpeace Co-Founder: No Scientific Proof Humans Are Dominant Cause Of Warming Climate." FoxNews.com. 26 February 2014. Taylor, James. "Global Warming Alarmists' Lame Outrage Highlights The Wisdom Of Charles Krauthammer." *Forbes*. 26 February 2014. Print

Krauthammer, Charles. "Charles Krauthammer: The Myth of 'Settled Science.'" *The Washington Post*. 20 February 2014. Print

Hollingsworth, Barbara. "Wrong: Al Gore Predicted Arctic Summer Ice Could Disappear In 2013." CNSNews.com. 13 September 2013

Michaels, Patrick J. and Paul C. Knappenberger. "Closing The Books On 2013: Another Year, Another Nail in the Coffin of Disastrous Global Warming." *Global Science Report*. Center For The Study of Science. 27 January 2014. Print

Knappenberger, Paul C. "US Carbon Dioxide Emissions Fall as Global Emissions Rise." *Global Science Report. Center for the Study of Science.* 10 June 2013. Print

Forbes, Viv. "Carbon Dioxide Can't Cause Wild Weird Weather." *American Thinker.* 19 February 2014. Print

Levinson, William A. "Climate Parasites: The Answer To 'Climate Change Deniers.'" *American Thinker.* 19 February 2014. Print

Singer, S. Fred. "Climate Consensus Con Game." *American Thinker.* 17 February 2014. Print

Bastasch, Michael. "Global Warming Gets Nearly Twice As Much Taxpayer Money as Border Security." *The Daily Caller.* 28 October 2013. Print

Wright, Dexter. "Climategate's stubborn Facts." *American Thinker.* 16 December 2009. Print

Singer, S. Fred. "Non-Governmental Climate Scientists Slam The UN's IPCC." *American Thinker.* 3 November 2013. Print

Wilson, Peter. "Warmists Pivot to Climate Adaptation." *American Thinker.* 22 January 2014. Print

Singer, S. Fred. "IPCC's Bogus Evidence For Global Warming." *American Thinker.* 12 November 2013. Print

United Nations Intergovernmental Panel on Climate Change. Assessment Report Number One. 1990. Print.

United Nations Intergovernmental Panel on Climate Change. Assessment Report Number Two. 1996. Print.

Moran, Rick. "Climate Scientist Faults Obama Science Advisor For 'Zombie Science.'" *American Thinker.* 16 February 2014. Print

United Nations Intergovernmental Panel on Climate Change. Assessment Report Number Three. 2001. Print.

United Nations Intergovernmental Panel on Climate Change. Assessment Report Number Four. 2007. Print.

Buckley, J.W. "If-By-Warming." *American Thinker.* 6 December 2013. Print

United Nations Intergovernmental Panel on Climate Change. Assessment Report Number Five. 2013. Print.

Non-Governmental International Panel on Climate Change. "Climate Change Reconsidered-II." 2013. Print.

Folks, Jeffrey. "Global Warming Gone AWOL." *American Thinker*. 20 December 2013. Print

Gaul, Ben. "Global Warming Causes Global Spending: Follow The Money." *Liberty Voice*. 17 January 2014. Print

Thorner, Nancy. "18 Facts to Combat Global Warming Scare Tactics." *Illinois Review*. 25 May 2012. Print

Lifson, Thomas. "EU Backing Away From Warmist Agenda." *American Thinker*. 20 January 2014. Print

"Ten Myths Of Global Warming." Globalwarminghysteria.com. 2013. Michaels, Patrick J. " Global warming Myth." *Washington Times*. 16 May 2008. Print

Hollingsworth, Barbara. "What Global Warming? 2012 Data Confirms Earth In Cooling Trend." *CNS News*. 13 August 2013. Print

Singer, S. Fred. "A Tale Of Two Climate Hockeysticks." *American Thinker*. 20 August 2013. Print

Singer, S. Fred. "The Inventor Of The Global Warming Hockey Stick Doubles Down." *American Thinker*. 21 January 2014. Print

Watts, Anthony. "New Study Suggests Global Warming Decreases Storm Activity And Extreme Weather." *Watts Up With That?* 25 January 2014. Print

Essex, Christopher. "Climate Bullies, The Surrealists Of Science." *American Thinker*. 9 December 2013. Print

Goddard, Steven. "U.S. Having its Coldest Six Month Period Since 1912." *Climate Depot*. 12 March 2014. Print

Goddard, Steven. "40 Year Anniversary Of Climate Experts Being Hysterical About Global Cooling." *Real Science*. 12 March 2014. Print

Markay, Lachlan. "Wikipedia Bans Radical Global Warming Propagandist From Editing All Pages." *NewsBusters*. 21 October 2010. Print

Delingpole, James. "Climategate: The Corruption Of Wikipedia." *The Telegraph*. 22 December 2009. Print

Jacobson, Paul. "My Two Favorite Questions For Global Warmists." *American Thinker*. 4 June 2014. Print

Cooke, Charles. "Climate Change Will Cause Rape and Murder and Assault and Robbery and Larceny and Make People Steal Your Car." *National Review Online*. 1 March 2014. Print

Morano, Marc. "UN IPCC Climate Report Untrustworthy." *Climate Depot*. 27 September 2013. Print

Idso, Craig D. et al. "Scientific Critique Of IPCC's 2013'Summary For Policymakers.'" 2013. Print.

Intergovernmental Panel on Climate Change. Summary For Policymakers. 27 September 2013. Print.

Long, Sean. "*NBC* Documentary Ignores Skeptics, Insists '97 Percent' Agree On Climate Change." Business And Media Institute. 8 April 2014. Print

Folks, Jeffrey. "2014: The Year Without Summer." *American Thinker*. 22 April 2014. Print

Bell, Larry. "Global Warming Alarmism: When Science Is Fiction." *Forbes*. 29 May 2012. Print

Taylor, James. "New NASA Data Blows Gaping Hole In Global Warming Alarmism." *Forbes*. 27 July 2011. Print

Rayne, Sierra. "Global Cooling Underway." *American Thinker*. 7 May 2014. Print

"The Antarctic Ice: The Other Side." *The Tribune Review*. 13 May 2014. Print

Williams, Walter. "Environmental Wackoism: We Are The Idiots." *Capitalism Magazine*. 21 May 2013. Print

Gaul, Ben. "Antarctica: Record Cold And Growing Ice Chills Global Warming Theories." *Liberty Voice*. 12 December 2013. Print

Samenow, Jason. "Antarctic Sea Ice Hit 35-Year Record High Saturday." *Washington Post*. 23 September 2013. Print

Gillis, Justin and Chang, Kenneth. "Scientists Warn of Rising Oceans From Polar Melt." *The New York Times*. 12 May 2104. Print

Watson, Traci. "Antarctic Glaciers Melting 'Passed Point Of No Return.'" *USA Today*. 13 May 2014. Print

Boyle, Alan. "Get a Reality Check On The Antarctic Meltdown and Rising Sea Level." *NBC News*. 13 May 2014

Bastasch, Michael. "Global Cooling: Antarctic Sea Ice Coverage Continues To Break Records." *The Daily Caller*. 13 May 2014. Print

Rejcek, Peter. "Sizzling September: More Weather Records Fall As South Pole Emerges From Long Winter." *Antarctic Sun*. 25 October 2013. Print

Morano, Marc. "UN Scientists Who Have Turned On The UN IPCC & Man-Made Climate Fears —A Climate Depot Flashback Report." *Climate Depot*. 21 August 2013

Morano, Marc. "Green Guru James Lovelock On Climate Change: 'I Don't Think Anybody Really Knows What's Happening. They Just Guess.' — Lovelock Reverses Himself On Global Warming." *Climate Depot*. 3 April 2014.

Sheahen, Dr. Tom. "The Specialized Meaning Of Words In The 'Antarctic Ice Shelf Collapse' And Other Climate Alarm Stories." *Watts Up With That*? 21 May 2014.

Homewood, Paul. "Misleading Hype Over Antarctic Ice Loss." *Climate Depot*. 21 May 2014.

"Study Falsely Classifies Scientists' Papers, According To The Scientists That Published Them." *Popular Technology.Net*. 21 May 2013.

Taylor, James. "Climate Alarmists Caught Doctoring '97 Percent Consensus' Claims." *Forbes*. 18 June 2013. Print

Rayne, Sierra. "Climate Models Fail." *American Thinker*. 11 May 2014. Print

Chapter Three

Williams, Walter. "Time For An Honest Examination Of Race. "*American Thinker*. 2 August 2013. Print

Sowell, Thomas. "Race-Hustling Results." *American Thinker*. 23 October 2013. Print

Locke, Edwin A. "What We Should Remember On Martin Luther King Day." *Capitalism Magazine*. 16 January 2014. Print

Marcus, Lloyd. "Liberal Media Gives Black Racism A Pass." *American Thinker*. 3 March 2011. Print

Cooke, Phil. " The Most Racist Part Of The Zimmerman Trial Was The Media." *Charisma News*. 16 July 2013. Print

Walsh, Dean. "Does The Western Media Ignore Anti-White Racism?" *World News Curator*. 22 August 2013. Print

United States Census Bureau. "Time Series: Seasonally Adjusted Home Ownership Rate." June 2014. Print.

United States. Bureau of Labor Statistics. "Consumer Price Index—All Urban Consumers." June 2014. Print.

Hustmyre, Chuck. "Modern American Racism." *American Thinker*. 5 April 2009. Print

De Hundehutte, Simon. "Race, The Race, And Racism." *American Thinker*. 30 August 2012. Print

Simon, Roger L. "The Democratic Party's War On Black People And How To Counter It." *PJ Media*. 25 March 2014. Print

DeMar, Gary. " Blacks As 'Chumps': Words From Malcom X." *Political Outcast*. 25 January 2013. Print

Agee, B. Christopher. "Democrats History Of Racism." Westernjournalism.com. 30 July 2012. Nelson, Sophia. "Should Black Folks Give The Tea Party A Second Look?" Freerepublic.com. 14 July 2010

United States Department Of Agriculture, Food and Nutrition Services. "Supplemental Nutrition Assistance Program. 6 June 2014. Print

Stanage, Niall. "Black Lawmakers Lament Flaring Of Racial Tensions Under Obama." *The Hill*. 26 August 2013. Print

Fenig, Ethel C. "The Democratic Party's Long History Of Racism." *American Thinker*. 15 October 2012. Print

Lifson, Thomas. "Calling Out Liberal Racism." *American Thinker*. 26 March 2014. Print

Bennett, John T. "Racism And The PC Inquisition." *American Thinker*. 17 May 2012. Print

Williams, Noel S. "The Tea Party Is Colorblind." *American Thinker*. 5 October 2013. Print

Perazzo, John. "Black Racism Rampant In America." Rense.com. 27 September 2007

Buchanan, Pat. "Black America's Real Problem Isn't White Racism." *Real Clear Politics*. 19 July 2013. Print

Jackson, Kevin. "The Zimmerman Case exposes Black Racism." *The Black Sphere. Free Republic*. 12 July 2013. Print

Peterson, Jesse Lee. "Black Racism Unchained." WorldNetDaily. Commentary. 26 December 2012. Marcus, Lloyd. "A Black-On-Black Discussion Of Black Racism." *American Thinker*. 16 January 2010. Print

Case, Mary Anne. "My Brother's Keeper Initiative Echoes Of A Sexist History." *The New York Times*. 12 March 2014. Print

Kalahar, Dean. "The Decline Of The African-American Family." *American Thinker*. 29 March 2014. Print

Gratz, Jennifer. "Discriminating Toward Equality: Affirmative Action And The Diversity Charade." The Heritage Foundation. 27 February 2014. Print

Smith, Rosslyn, "Prominent Blacks Deserting The Liberal Plantation." *American Thinker*. 25 June 2013. Print

Thurler, Kim. "Reverse Racism: Whites Believe They Are Victims Of Racism More Often Than Blacks." *Medical News Today*. 24 May 2011. Print

Parker, Pete. "Black racism: The Evil Of Our Time." Clashdaily.com. 3 September 2013.

Nolte, John. "Media Target The Powerless; Protect Powerful Liars, Bigots and Race Hoaxers." *Breitbart. Big Journalism*. 14 August 2013. Print

Pollak, Joel B. "Politico: Republicans Better At 'Diversity' Than Democrats." *Breitbart. Big Journalism*. 15 August 2013. Print

Munro, Neil. "Poll; Race Relations Have Plummeted Since Obama Took Office." *The Daily Caller.* July 2013. Print

Richardson, Diane. "Behavior, Power And Control, Racism And Playing The N Word Game." *American Thinker.* 19 August 2013. Print

Beatty, W. A. " Democrats Continue To Prove That It's All about Vote-Buying." *American Thinker.* 12 August 2013. Print

"A Short History Of Democrats, Republicans, And Racism." *RussP.us.* 2011. Bartlett, Bruce. "Wrong On Race: The Democrat Party's Buried Past. New York: Palgrave Macmillan, 2008. Print.

Owens, Mackubin T. "The Democratic Party's Legacy Of Racism." Ashbrook Center At Ashland University. December 2002. Print.

United States Department Of Labor, Bureau Of Labor Statistics. Current Population Survey. "Employment Situation." Washington, DC. June 2014. Print.

Desmond-Harris, Jenee. "White People Face The Worst Racism." *The Root.* 23 May 2011. Print

DeBroux, Louis. "History Of Democrat Racism. . . Hope And Chains." *UnitedLiberty.org.* 21 August 2012. United States Department Of Labor, Bureau Of Labor Statistics. Current Population Survey. "Employment Situation." Washington, DC. May 2014. Print.

Toplansky, Eileen F. "Obama Promotes Racism." *American Thinker.* 19 August 2013. Print.

"Race And Ethnicity" Poll. PollingReport.com. August 2013United States Department Of Agriculture, Food and Nutrition Services. "Supplemental Nutrition Assistance Program. 6 June 2014. Print

"Transcript: President Obama Addresses Race, Profiling and Florida Law." *CNN Politics.* 19 July 2013. Print

United States Department Of Labor, Bureau Of Labor Statistics. Current Population Survey. "Employment Situation." Washington, DC. December 2008. Print.

Moran, Rick. "If Jesse Jackson Says So, It Has To Be True." *American Thinker.* 24 August 2013. Print

Fenig, Ethel C. "The Roar Of Sharpton's And Obama's Non Reaction To The Lane Murder." *American Thinker.* 24 August 2013. Print

Opelka ,Mike. "Another Senseless Murder You're Not Hearing about—And Some In The Family Wonder If It Could Be A Trayvon Martin Revenge Murder." Theblaze.com. 22 August 2013. United States Department Of Labor, Bureau Of Labor Statistics. Current Population Survey. "Employment Situation." Washington, DC. July 2014. Print.

Harris, James T. "When Racists Are Right." *The National Conversation*. 14 June 2007. Print

McCain, Robert Stacy. "How A Miami School Crime Cover-up Policy Led To Trayvon Martin's Death." *The American Spectator*. 15 July 2013. Print

Ross, Doug. "Trayvon Martin's Drug Abuse: Lean/Purple Drank and DXM (A PCP-Like Substance)." *Doug Ross@Journal*. 14 July 2013.

United States Department Of Labor, Bureau Of Labor Statistics. Current Population Survey. "Employment Situation." Washington, DC. January 2009. Print.

Korwin, Alan. "Trayvon Martin: The True Story Leaks Out." *The Hot Spot*. 4 October 2013. Print

Cunningham, Todd. "Trayvon Martin Tape Editing Prompts Internal Probe At *NBC* (Report)." *The Wrap*. 1 April 2012. Print

Byler, David. "Poll: Obama Approval Rating At New Low." *Real Clear Politics*. 6 August 2014. Print

United States Department Of Labor, Bureau Of Labor Statistics. Current Population Survey. "Employment Situation." Washington, DC. September 2014. Print.

United States Department Of Labor, Bureau Of Labor Statistics. Current Population Survey. "Employment Situation." Washington, DC. September 2013. Print.

United States Department Of Labor, Bureau Of Labor Statistics. Current Population Survey. "Employment Situation." Washington, DC. August 2014. Print.

Chapter Four

United States Bureau of Justice Statistics: National Crime Victimization Survey (2012)

Kleck, Gary and Gertz, Marc. "Armed Resistance to Crime: The Prevalence and Nature of Self-Defense with a Gun," *The Journal of Criminal Law & Criminology*, Northwestern University School of Law, Volume 86, Number 1.

Kleck, Gary and Gertz, Marc. National Self Defense Survey (1993)

Cook, Philip J. and Ludwig, Jenz. "Guns In America: National Survey On Private Ownership and Use of Firearms." *National Institute of Justice*. 1997. Print

Leghorn, Nick. "Debunking 'A Dummy's Guide to Winning Gun Control Debates'" *The Truth About Guns.* 2013: Print

Sullivan, William. "Weighing The Gun Control Argument." *American Thinker*. 24 February 2013. Print

Trinko, Tom. "Why Liberals Support Gun Control." *American Thinker*. 13 April 2013. Print

Paltzik, Edward. "The Fallacy Of Gun Control." *American Thinker*. 1 January 2013. Print

Bureau of Alcohol Tobacco Firearms and Explosives: Firearms Commerce In The United States (PDF)

Moseley, Jonathon. "Gun Control Derangement Syndrome." *American Thinker*. 15 April 2013. Print

Lott Jr., Dr. John R. "Media Silence Is Deafening About Important Gun News." FoxNews.com. 30 September 2011.

Lott Jr., John R. ed." More Guns, Less Crime." Third ed. Chicago: University of Chicago Press, 2010. Print.

Rodriguez, Andrew. "Experts Disagree on Mental Health's Role In Shootings." *The Red Line Project*. 6 March 2013. Print

Phelan, John. "The Costs Of Gun Control." *The Commentator*. 18 December 2012. Print

"China Knife Attack: Teen Reportedly Kills 8, Wounds 5 In Northeast." *Beijing. World Post*. 2 August 2012. Print

Piccione, Mike. "Adam Lanza Evidence List Includes Probable Weapon In Mother's Murder." *The Daily Caller*. 28 March 2013. Print.

Federal Bureau of Investigation, Uniform Crime Report In The United States. 2011. Print.

National Vital Statistics Reports Centers For Disease Control, Washington. D.C. Volumes 47- 63. 1998 – 2013. Print

Sowell, Thomas. "Do Gun Control Laws Control Guns?" *Town Hall Daily*. 22 January 2013. Print

Thomas, Trevor. "Some Inconvenient Truths About American Mass Murderers." *American Thinker*. 12 June 2014. Print

Lord, Jeffrey. "Gun Control Won't Stop The Next Elliot Rodger." *American Spectator*. 27 May 2014. Print

Duke, Selwyn. "How Covering Up Minority Crime Leads To Gun Control." *American Thinker.* 6 June 2014. Print

Federal Bureau of Information Uniform Crime Reports, Crime In The United States. 2005. Print.

Resolution 2117. United Nations Security Council. 7036th Meeting. New York. 26 September 2013. Print

Krouse, William. "How Many Guns Are In The United States?" Gun Control Legislation; United States Congressional Research Service, Washington D.C. 14 November 2012. Print

Hoyert, Donna L. and Xu, Jiaquan. "Deaths: Preliminary Data For 2011— Selected Causes." National Vital Statistics Reports, Hyattsville, MD; U.S. Department Of Health And Human Services, Centers For Disease Control, Division Of Vital Statisics. 10 October 2012. Print

United Nations Office on Drugs and Crime. "Homicides And Gun Homicides In The United States." Global study on Homicide 2013. Vienna. 10 April 2014. Print

United Nations Office on Drugs and Crime. "Homicide in 207 Countries—United States." Global study on Homicide 2011. Vienna. United Nations Office on Drugs and Crime. 26 June 2013. Print

Federal Bureau Of Investigation. "Crime In The United States." Uniform Crime Reports. Washington. 29 January 2013. Print

United States Bureau of Alcohol, Tobacco, Firearms and Explosives. "Annual Firearms Manufacturing and Export Report; Year 2012." 17 Jan 2014. Print

United States Bureau of Alcohol, Tobacco, Firearms and Explosives. "Annual Firearms Manufacturing and Export Report; Year 2008." 8 Mar 2011. Print

Cook, Philip J. and Ludwig, Jens. "The Limited Impact Of The Brady Act— No Evidence Of Reduction In Deaths." Reducing Gun Violence In America: Informing Policy with Evidence and Analysis. Baltimore, MD. Johns Hopkins University Press. 25 January 2013. Print

Jacoby, Jeff. "Crime Soared with Mass. Gun Law." *Globe*. 17 February 2013. Print

Howerton, Jason. "The Firearms Statistics That Gun Control Advocates Don't Want To See." *The Blaze*. 6 May 2013. Print

Strieff (Diary). "Chicago's Murder Rate Plummets With Concealed Carry Law." *Red State*. 4 April 2014. Print

Chapter Five

Fleischman, Jon. "Univision Survey: Immigration Low Priority For Latino Voters In California." *Breitbart*. 8 August 2014. Print

Boyle, Matthew. "Experts: Ebola Could Cross Unsecured U.S. Border." *Breitbart*. 8 August 2014

Rector, Robert and Christine Kim. " The Fiscal Cost Of Low-Skill Immigrants To The U.S. Taxpayer." Heritage Foundation. Robert Rector Testimony before the subcommittee on Immigration of the committee on the Judiciary of the United States House Of Representatives. Washington D,C. 17 May 2007. Print

Bennett, John. "America's Never-Ending Shame: Importing Inequality." *American Thinker*. 17 May 2014. Print

"Immigration, Poverty and Low-Wage Earners: The Harmful Effect Of Unskilled Immigrants on American Workers." Federation For American Immigration Reform. 2011. Print.

Pelner Cosman, Madeleine. "Illegal Aliens And American Medicine." *Journal Of American Physicians and Surgeons*. Volume 10 Number 1. 2005. Print.

Chong, J.R. "Hawthorne Hospital to shut doors. R.F. Kennedy Medical Center cites financial problems for closure. Sixth ER in LA County this year." *Los Angeles Times*. 24 September 2004. Print

Wright CM. "SSI: The black hole of the welfare state." Cato Policy Analysis 224, April 1995. Print

Garrett, L. *The Coming Plague*. New York, N.Y.: Penguin. 1995. Print

United States Government Accountability Office. "Criminal Alien Statistics." GAO-11-187. March 2011. Print

Federation For American Immigration Reform. "Criminal Aliens." 2012. Print

Martin, Jack and Ruark, Erick A. "The Fiscal Burden of Illegal Immigration on United States Taxpayers," *FAIR*. July 2010: Print

Munro, Neil. "Arrested illegals who were released charged with 16,226 subsequent crimes," *Daily Caller*. 9 August 2012. Print

Noble, Sara. "37,007 Criminal Aliens Released Last Year So We Can Stand For Love." *American Thinker*. 26 August 2014. Print

Pavlich, Katie. "Hundreds More Criminal Illegal Aliens With Brutal Records Released Onto American Streets." *Town Hall*. 15 August 2014. Print

Berger, Judson. "Enforcement 'Crisis'? Documents Show 68,000 'Criminal Aliens' Released Last Year." FoxNews.com. 31 March 2014.

"Border Patrol Union Claims The U.S. Is Letting People Into The Country With Known Ties To Gangs." *America's Watchtower*. 14 June 2014. Print

Lee, Tony. "Texas State Senator: 100,000 Illegal Immigrant Gang Members In State." *Breitbart*. 21 July 2014. Print

"Study: 1 Million Sex Crimes By Illegals" *WorldNetDaily*. 31 May 2006. Print

Potter, Mark. "Illegal Drugs Flow Over And Under U.S. Border." *NBC News*. Nogales, AZ. 22 October 2009. Print

Starnes, Todd. "Immigration Crisis: Tuberculosis Spreading At Camps." FoxNews.com. 7 July 2014. Wagner, P.F. "The Dark Side Of Illegal Immigration." www.usillegalaliens.com. 2007

Melton, Melissa. "Infectious Disease Outbreaks Tied to Illegal Immigrant Influx." *The Daily Sheeple*. 21 June 2014. Print

Herriman, Robert. "Dengue Fever In The Americas: 1 Million Cases And Counting." *Outbreak News Today.* 2 September 2014. Print

United States Centers For Disease Control and Prevention, Arboviral Diseases Branch. "West Nile virus disease cases and deaths reported to CDC by year and clinical presentation." 1999-2013. Print

Bellinger, Lee. "Third World Diseases Making a Comeback In The USA Via Illegal Immigrants." *Independent Living.* 15 August 2012. Print

United States Department Of Health and Human Services, Health Resources And Services Administration. "New U.S. Reported Hansen's Disease (Leprosy) Cases By Year." 1979-2009. Print

Thomas, Cal. "Retreating On Illegal Immigration." Townhall.com. 4 February 2014

Adams, T. Becket. "Poll: Almost Twice As Many Americans Want A Decrease In Immigration As Want An Increase." *Washington Examiner.* 27 June 2014. Print

Richards, Greg. "A Nation Of Immigrants." *American Thinker.* 13 July 2014. Print

Walker, Bruce. "The Answer To Our Immigration Problem." *American Thinker.* 26 June 2014. Print

Camarota, Steven A. and Zeigler, Karen. "All Employment Growth Since 2000 Went To Immigrants. Number Of U.S. Born Not Working Grew By 17 Million." Center For Immigration Studies. June 2014. Print

"New Report Claims That ISIS Is Operating In Mexico." *America's Watchtower.* 29 August 2014. Print

Borjas, George J. et al. "Immigration And African-American Employment Opportunities: The Response Of Wages, Employment, And Incarceration To Labor Supply Shocks." National Bureau of Economic Research. Working Paper 12518. Cambridge,MA. September 2006. Print .

McHam, Gerren. "The Big Immigration Problem No One's Talking About." *The Daily Signal.* 15 May 2014. Print

Bennett, John. "Where Is America's Sense Of Self-Preservation?" *American Thinker.* 9 June 2014. Print

"Flood Of Illegal Immigrant Children Into Texas Costing U.S. Taxpayers Billions." *News Radio 1200 WOAI.* San Antonio. 2 June 2014.

Rector, Robert and Richwine, Erick A., PH.D. "The Fiscal Cost Of Unlawful Immigrants And Amnesty To The U.S. Taxpayer." Heritage Foundation. 6 May 2013. Print

Kane, Tim, PH.D. and Johnson, Kirk A., PH.D. "The Real Problem With Immigration . . . And The Real Solution." Heritage Foundation. 1 March 2006. Print

Van Son, Gene M. "A Sane Immigration Policy." *American Thinker.* 10 March 2014. Print

Naik, Abhijit. "Impacts Of Illegal Immigration." *Buzzle.* 10 October 2011. Print

Brimelow, Peter. *Alien Nation: Common Sense About America's Immigration Disaster.* New York: Random House, 1995. Print.

United States Federal Bureau of Investigation Uniform Crime Reports, Crime In The United States. 2005. Print.

Seper, Jerry. "Illegal Criminal Aliens Abound In U.S." *Washington Times.* January 2004. Print

MacDonald, Heather. "The Illegal-Alien Crime Wave." *City Journal.* Winter 2004. Print.

Thiess, Heidi. "Mexican Gunmen Involved In Arizona Border Incident Actually Uniformed Mexican Force." *Euphoric Reality.* 8 January 2007. Print

Lifson, Thomas. "Report: 125,000 Illegals In California Qualified To Be Covered By Medicaid." *American Thinker.* 26 February 2014. Print

Moseley, Jonathan. "Amnesty: Not Just For Low-Skilled Workers?" *American Thinker.* 24 February 2014. Print

Charette, Robert N. "The STEM Crisis Is A Myth." *Spectrum.* 30 August 2013. Print

Bennett, John. "Eric Cantor Versus The Founders On Immigration." *American Thinker.* 1 February 2014. Print

Malanga, Steven. "How Unskilled Immigrants Hurt Our Economy." *City Journal.* Summer 2006. Print.

United States House Of Representatives. Immigration And Nationality Act Of 1965. Passed 25 August 1965. Print.

Chapter Six

"Facts About Minimum Wage." Heritage Foundation. Factsheet #136. 30 January 2014. Print

Sowell, Thomas. "Minimum Wage Madness." *Jewish World Review.* 17 September 2013. Print

Morison, Katie. "Govt Aid Pays More Than A Minimum-Wage Job In 35 States." *MSN News.* 22 August 2013

Marcus, Lloyd. "Democrats' Immoral Approach To Minimum Wage." *American Thinker.* 7 May 2014. Print

Hellner, Jack. "Minimum Wage: Denying Opportunity." *American Thinker.* 31 May 2014. Print

Berman, Richard. "Why Unions Want A Higher Minimum Wage." *Wall Street Journal.* 25 February 2013. Print.

Merline, John. "Minimum Wage Hike Support Falls On CBO Jobs Warning." *Investors Business Daily.* 27 February 2014. Print

Perry, Mark J. "Two More Reasons Raising The Minimum Wage Is A Bad Idea." *Economic Policy Journal.* 2 March 2014. Print

Ekins, Emily. "Americans Will Only Support Obama's Minimum Wage Increases If It Doesn't Harm Jobs." Reason.com. 28 January 2014. Davis, Sean. "11 Facts Obama Forgot To Mention About Minimum Wage." *Media Trackers.* 29 January 2014. Print

Burguiere, Stu. "Americans Love The Minimum Wage, Unless You Tell Them The Truth About It." *The Blaze.* 13 February 2014. Print

United States Department of Health and Human Services. 2014 Poverty Guidelines. January 2014. Print.

Sabia, Joseph J. "Minimum Wages: A Poor Way To Reduce Poverty." Cato Institute. Tax and Budget Bulletin Number 70. March 2014. Print.

Vaca, Chris. "Obama and The Minimum Wage." *Conservative Daily News.* 17 February 2014. Print

"The Real History Behind The Minimum Wage (HINT: It Involves Progressives And Eugenics)." *The Blaze.* 14 February 2014. Print

"How The Federal Minimum Wage Crushed The Economy of American Samoa." Cleveland.com. 18 October 2012.

Sherk, James. "What Is Minimum Wage: It's History And Effects On The Economy." Heritage Foundation. Testimony before Health, Education, Labor And Pensions Committee, United States Senate. 25 June 2013. Print.

United States Government Accountability Office. *"American Samoa and the Commonwealth of the Northern Mariana Islands: Employment, Earnings, and Status of Key Industries Since Minimum Wage Increases Began."* Report No. GAO-11-427, June 2011. Print

U.S. Department of Labor. *"Impact of Increased Minimum Wages on the Economies of American Samoa and the Commonwealth of the Northern Mariana Islands."* January 2008.

Neumark, David; Salas, Ian; and Wascher, William. "Revisiting the Minimum Wage Employment Debate: Throwing Out the Baby with the Bathwater?" National Bureau of Economic Research. Working Paper No. 18681. 2013. Print.

McMorris, Bill. "CBO: Minimum Wage Hike Could Leave 1 Million Unemployed." *The Washington Free Beacon*. 18 February 2014. Print

Bandow, Doug. "The Minimum Wage: Immoral And Inefficient." Cato Institute. 14 January 2014. Print

Dorn, James A. "The Minimum Wage Is Cruelest To Those Who Can't Find a Job." Forbes.com. 22 July 2013

Saltsman, Michael. "The Record Is Clear: Minimum Wage Hikes Destroy Jobs." Employment Policies Institute. 17 April 2013. Print

Dorn, James A. "Mr. President, Increasing The Minimum Wage Is Wrong Medicine For Ailing Economy." Cato Institute. 22 January 2014. Print

Jeffrey, Terry. "Minimum Wage Hike Attacks Young And Industrious." Townhall.com. 19 February 2014

Adams, Becket. "CBO: Of Course Raising The Minimum Wage Will Eliminate Jobs (Guess By How Much)." *The Blaze*. 18 February 2014. Print

Lifson, Thomas. "CBO confirms Dem Minimum Wage Hike Will Cost At Least Half a Million Jobs." *American Thinker*. 19 February 2014. Print

Saltsman, Michael. "Increasing Minimum Wage Would Impact Employment." Employment Policies Institute. 17 April 2013. Print

Beatty, W.A. "The Minimum Wage Issue . . . Again." *American Thinker*. 21 December 2013. Print

Wilson, Mark. "The Negative Effects Of Minimum Wage Laws." Cato Institute. September 2012. Print.

United States Department of Labor, Wage and Hour Division. "Minimum Wage Laws in the States." 1 January 2012. Print.

Saltsman, Michael. "Minimum Wage Hikes Cost Teens Jobs." Employment Policies Institute. 28 May 2013. Print

United States Bureau of Labor Statistics. "Characteristics of Minimum Wage Workers: 2010." 25 February 2011. Print.

Unites States House Committee on Natural Resources, Subcommittee on Fisheries, Wildlife, Oceans and Insular Affairs. Governor Togiola Tulafono, testimony: "The Impact of Minimum Wage Increases on American Samoa." 23 September 2011. Print.

Burkhauser , Richard V. and Sabia, Joseph J. "The Effectiveness of Minimum Wage Increases in Reducing Poverty: Past, Present, and Future." *Contemporary Economic Policy* 25. April 2007. Print.

Hearne, Samuel. "Minimum Wage Law Backfires In American Samoa." Featured, *The Economy*. 6 July 2011. Print

Chapter Seven

Ryan, Frank. "The Real Employment Problem." *American Thinker*. 16 November 2013. Print

Street, Chriss. "Only Private Sector Stimulates Job Growth." *American Thinker*. 9 December 2013. Print

Bedard, Paul. "Wall Street Advisor: Actual Unemployment is 37.2%, 'Misery Index' Worst In 40 Years." *The Examiner*. 21 January 2014. Print

Harrington, Elizabeth. "Employers Say Obamacare Will Cost Them $5,000 More Per Employee*." The Washington Free Beacon*. 2 April 2014. Print

United States Bureau Of Labor Statistics, Current Population Survey. "How The Government Measures Unemployment." June 2014. Print.

Teichman, Brent. "Understanding The Unemployment Numbers." WordPress.com. 7 February 2011

Bell, Chris W. "Understanding Unemployment Statistics." *American Thinker*. 8 February 2012. Print

United States Department Of Labor, Bureau Of Labor Statistics, Current Population Survey: "Employment Situation." Washington, DC. September 2014. Print.

Meyer, Ali. "Record Number Of Americans Not In Labor Force In June." CNSNews.com. 3 July 2014.

Blake, Aaron. "Either Obama Is The Worst President Since World War II, Or Americans Just Have Really Short Memories." *The Washington Post*. 2 July 2014. Print

United States Department Of Labor, Bureau Of Labor Statistics, Current Population Survey. ""Employment Situation."" Washington, DC. September 2013. Print.

McMahon, Timothy. "Current U-6 Unemployment Rate Is 11.8% BLS and 16.6% Gallup." Unemployment Data.com. 2 May 2014.

Stransky, Brenton. "The Truth About The Unemployment Rate In 2 Graphs." *American Thinker*. 10 September 2012. Print

McMahon, Timothy. "Is The Government Fudging Unemployment Numbers?" UnemploymentData.com. 2 May 2014

United States Department Of Labor, Bureau Of Labor Statistics, Current Population Survey. "Employment Situation." Washington, DC. August 2014. Print.

Jackson, Brooks. "Obama's Numbers (July 2014 Update)." FactCheck.org. 8 July 2014

Saltsman, Michael. "Increasing Minimum Wage Would Impact Employment." Employment Policies Institute. 17 April 2013. Print

Butrick, Richard. "Bursting With Pride (And Ignorance)." *American Thinker*. 26 July 2014. Print

Sorenson, Otto. "Behind The BLS Unemployment Numbers." *American Thinker*. 6 October 2012. Print

United States Department Of Labor, Bureau Of Labor Statistics, Current Population Survey. ""Employment Situation."" Washington, DC. July 2014. Print.

Gestetner, Yossi. "The 7.8% Unemployment Rate in Context." *Conservative Underground*. 8 October 2012. Print

Moran, Rick. "Official Unemployment Rate Drops But Broader Jobless Measure Rises." *American Thinker*. 3 May 2013. Print

Moran, Rick. "Obama Echoes Pelosi —Unemployment Benefits Create Jobs." *American Thinker*. 9 December 2011. Print

United States Department Of Labor, Bureau Of Labor Statistics, Current Population Survey. "Employment Situation." Washington, DC. June 2014. Print.

Carson, Jonathan David. "Another Misleading Unemployment Statistic." *American Thinker*. 30 August 2013. Print

Saltsman, Michael. "The Record Is Clear: Minimum Wage Hikes Destroy Jobs." *Employment Policies Institute*. 17 April 2013. Print

Hoven, Randall. "Un-Spinning Jobs Numbers." *American Thinker*. 10 September 2012. Print

United States Department Of Labor, Bureau Of Labor Statistics. Current Population Survey. "Employment Situation." Washington, DC. May 2014. Print.

Limbaugh, David. "Liberal Myths On Unemployment." *GOP USA*. 10 January 2014. Print

Kiely, Eugene and Farley, Robert. "Obama's Economic Sleight Of Hand." *FactCheck.org*. 15 June 2012. Print

United States Department Of Labor, Bureau Of Labor Statistics. Current Population Survey. "Employment Situation." Washington, DC. January 2009. Print.

United States Department Of Labor, Bureau Of Labor Statistics. Current Population Survey. "Employment Situation." Washington, DC. December 2008. Print.

Jeffrey, Terence P. "86M Full-Time Private-Sector Workers Sustain 148M Benefit Takers." Townhall.com. 16 April 2014

Starr, Penny. "Summertime Blues: Teen Unemployment In Major U.S. Cities Tops 50 Percent." CNSNews.com. 2 June 2014.

Saltsman, Michael. "Minimum Wage Hikes Cost Teens Jobs." Employment Policies Institute. 28 May 2013. Print

Sabia, Joseph J. " The Effect of Minimum Wage Increases On Retail and Small Business employment." Employment Policies Institute. 2006. Print.

United States National Assessment Of Adult Literacy, Department Of Education, National Center For Education Statistics. 2003. Print.

Neumark, David. "Minimum Wage In The Post-welfare Reform Era." Employment Policies Institute. 2007. Print.

Meyer, Ali. "37.2%: Percentage Not In Labor Force Remains At 36-Year High." CNSNews.com. 6 June 2014

Halper, Daniel. "For Every Person Added To Labor Force, 10 Added To Those Not In Labor Force." *The Weekly Standard*. 15 October 2012. Print

Moran, Rick. "Jobs Numbers: The Real Story." *American Thinker*. 17 March 2014. Print

"Average Unemployment Rate Higher Under Obama." *Net Advisor*. 16 June 2014. Meyer, Ali. "Record 55,553,000 Women Not Participating In Labor Force." CNSNews.com. 3 October 2014

Chapter Eight

Rector, Robert and Sheffield, Rachel. "Understanding Poverty In The United States: Surprising Facts About America's Poor." Heritage Foundation. Poverty And Inequality. 13 September 2011. Print

Brown, Jeffrey T. "Income Inequality: The Left's Next Big Con." *American Thinker*. 17 January 2014. Print

Moran, Rick. "Why Obama's Obsession With 'Inequality' Is Misguided." *American Thinker*. 23 December 2013. Print

Hagopian, Kip and Ohanian, Lee. "The Mismeasure Of Inequality." Hoover Institution. Policy Review. 1 August 2012. Print

Rector, Robert and Hederman, Jr., Rea S. "Income Inequality: How Census Data Misrepresent Income Distribution." Heritage Foundation. 29 September 1999. Print

Chantrill, Christopher. "Let's Talk About Inequality, Liberals." *American Thinker*. 8 August 2012. Print

Moran, Rick. "7 Reasons Why Obama Is Wrong About Income Inequality." *American Thinker*. 27 October 2011. Print

U.S. Census Bureau Current Population Surveys 1997-2012. Print.

McCann, Steve. "The Income Gap Con Game." *American Thinker*. 24 August 2011. Print

Hollingsworth, Barbara. "Study Finds Highest Income Inequality In Cities That Voted For Obama." CNSNews.com. 5 March 2014

Stossel, John. "Popular Nonsense." Townhall.com. 4 June 2014

U.S. Census Bureau; Selected Characteristics of Households by Total Money Income. 2102-HINC-01. 2012. Print.

Chapter Nine

"Infection Associated With Abortion." *Abortionrisks.org. Detrimental Effects of Abortion, An Annotated Bibliography*. Updated 10 March 2014. "Induced Abortion." The American College of Obstetricians and Gynecologists. 2001. Print

Paul M, et al. *A Clinician's Guide to Medical and Surgical Abortion*. New York: Churchill Livingstone. 1999. Print.

Creinin, Mitchell D. MD, et al. "Medical Management of Abortion." *American Journal of Obstetrics and Gynecology Practice*. Bulletin, no. 26. 2001. Print.

"Abortion Procedures." *American Pregnancy Association*. Updated July 2014. Print.

Hern, Warren M. *Abortion Practice*. Philadelphia: J. B. Lippincott Company, 1990. Print.

Downs, Rebecca. "Abortion Methods and Abortion Procedures Used To Kill Unborn Babies." LifeNews.com. 2 January 2013. Print

Schwarzwalder, Rob. "The Best Pro-Life Arguments For Secular Audiences." Family Research Council. Accessed June 2014. Print.

Moore, Keith L. and Persaud, T.V.N. *The Developing Human: Clinically Oriented Embryology*. Philadelphia: W.B. Saunders Co. 1998. Print.

"Fetal Development." *MedlinePlus*. US National Library Of Medicine. Updated 2 October 2014. Print.

Klusendorf, Scott. "How To Defend Your Pro-Life Views In 5 Minutes Or Less." Life Training Institute. Accessed July 2014. Print.

Walker, Bruce. "Abortion Polls And Hidden Conservatism." *American Thinker*. 27 May 2014. Print

Sullivan, William. "Tactically Tackling Abortion." *American Thinker*. 25 August 2012. Print

Williamson, Kevin D. "The Symbol Of a Lie." *National Review*. 22 March 2014. Print

Terzo, Sarah. "Nurse Describes Abortion Of a 'Miniature Human Being.'" Live Action News. 26 April 2014. Evenson, Darrick. "Dr. Martin Luther King, Jr. Had Pro-Life View Opposing Abortion." LifeNews.com. 22 July 2011

Childress, Clenard. "When Is A Racist A Racist? Abortion." *Renew America*. 19 July 2008. Print

Crouse, Janice Shaw. "Pro-Life Movement Victorious At Curbing Abortions." *American Thinker*. 4 February 2014. Print

Daveport, Mary L., MD. "New Study From China Helps To Prove The Abortion-Breast Cancer Link." *American Thinker*. 2 December 2013. Print

Huang, Yubei et al. "A Meta-Analysis Of The Association Between Induced Abortion And Breast Cancer Risk Among Chinese Females." *Cancer Causes And Control*. November 2013. Print.

United States Centers For Disease Control And Prevention. Data and Statistics. Abortion. 2010. Print.

"Facts On Induced Abortion In The United States." Guttmacher Institute. October 2013. Print.

"Abortion Risks, Abortion Dangers, and Abortion Complications." Ramah International. Accessed December 2013. Print.

"U.S. Abortion Statistics." Abort73.com. 28 November 2012. Accessed July 2014. "Abortion Risks." Abort73.com. 28 November 2012. Accessed July 2014. "Researcher Finally Admits Abortion Raises Breast Cancer Risk In Study That Fingers Oral Contraceptives As A Probable Cause Of Breast Cancer." *Medical News Today*. 7 January 2010. Print.

Stanek, Jill. "Top Scientist Finally Admits Abortion-Breast Cancer Link." *World Net Daily*. 13 January 2010

Johnson, Kate. "Induced Abortions Linked To Preterm Delivery." *Ob. Gyn. News*. December 2010. Print.

"The After Effects Of Abortion." AbortionFacts.com. Accessed July 2014. Diaz, Mario. "Who Wants To Be Pro-Choice?" *American Thinker*. 19 August 2013. Print

Spiering, Charlie. "Poll: 62% Of Americans Believe Abortion Is Morally Wrong." *Washington Examiner*. 22 January 2014. Print

Chapter Ten

Kessler, Glenn. "President Obama's Persistent '77-cent' Claim On The Wage Gap Gets A New Pinocchio Rating." *Washington Post*. 9 April 2014. Print

Scheurer, Jason. "The 77-Cent Gender Wage Gap Lie." *Breitbart*. 17 March 2014. Print

Sommers, Christina Hoff. "No, Women Don't Make Less Money Than Men." *The Daily Beast*. 1 February 2014. Print

Mirza, Syed Kamran. "Islamic Sharia Law In Brief." *Australian Islamic Monitor*. 5 February 2011. Print

Fiorina, Carly. "Here's Why Democrats' Phony 'War On Women' Won't Work." FoxNews.com. 19 August 2014.

Schlapp, Mercedes. "The Real War On Women." *U.S. News And World Report*. 16 August 2014. Print

Bargo, Michael, Jr. "The Democratic Party's War On Women." *American Thinker*. 5 June 2014. Print

Greszler, Rachel and Sherk, James. "Equal Pay For Equal Work: Examining The Gender Gap." Heritage Foundation. Issue Brief #4227. 22 May 2014. Print

United States Department of Labor, Bureau of Labor Statistics. "National Census of Fatal Occupational Injuries in 2012." Table 4, 22 August 2013. Print.

CONSAD Research. "An Analysis of the Reasons for the Disparity in Wages Between Men and Women." Final report prepared for the United States Department of Labor. January 2009. Print.

DeAngelis, Jeannie. "The Delicious Irony Of Hillary's Potential Political Demise." *American Thinker*. 23 june 2014. Print

Jones, Alex. "Cruz And Paul turn Up The Heat On Democratic Establishment." Infowars.com. 7 February 2014

DeMar, Gary. "Women Are The Casualties Of The Democrats' War On Women." *Godfather Politics.* 23 August 2012. Print

Lifson, Thomas. "Rand Paul Calls Out Democrat 'GOP War On Women' Hypocrisy." *American Thinker*. 27 January 2014. Print

Hoffman, Bill. "Huckabee: Democrats' 'War On Women' Claim Demeans Females." Newsmax.TV. 20 January 2014. DeMar, Gary. "Democrat War On Women: Let Me Count The Ways." *Godfather Politics*. 5 August 2013. Print

Beatty, Warren. "Democratic 'Equal Pay' Hypocrisy." *American Thinker*. 15 April 2014. Print

Jeffrey, Terence. "Only 38.6% Of Jobs Added Under Obama Have Gone To Women." CNSNews.com. 4 April 2014. Meyer, Ali. "180,000 More Women Unemployed In March." CNSNews.com. 4 April 2014

Sowell, Thomas. "Statistical Frauds: War On Women." *Capitalism Magazine*. 19 April 2014. Print